Perspectives

Kirk House Publishers

Perspectives

Building meaningful
connections by learning 4 steps
to courageously speak up

A self-guided journey by
Kendra Q. Dodd, MHRD

Paperback ISBN: 9781952976339

LCCN: 2021922499

Cover and interior design by Ann Aubitz

First Printing: November 2021

First Edition

Published by Kirk House Publishers
1250 E 115th Street
Burnsville, MN 55337
Kirkhousepublishers.com
612-781-2815

Acknowledgments

To my father, the late Phil Johnson, and my mother, Sandra Scott Johnson, for instilling in me the responsibility to serve. Through my parent's humbleness to educate, serve, and defend, I got the best of the two of you with your passions.

To my godmother, who treated me as her own, and pushed me to walk bridges that I was reluctant to courageously cross.

To my husband Milton, who has never questioned me in my journey and who has supported me, nonetheless.

To my children, who have given me even more reason to have no regret about my responsibility to make a difference.

To my brother, the first person to help teach me the responsibility of leadership.

To my village, you have supported me in various ways; I appreciate each of you! Especially Hillery and Deb, for the consistent feedback and my countless request for an opinion.

To all the rejections, challenges, and obstacles in my life that taught me relevancy, and enhanced my ability to impact this world.

To my publisher, Kirk House Publishers; you gracefully managed it all, dealing with my plethora of questions, my passionate nature and overall naivety—you are truly appreciated.

To my editors, Connie Anderson, Words and Deeds, Inc. and Lynn Garthwaite—I'm humbled by the patience and guidance. You all were the answered prayer that led me to the finish line.

To my beta-readers, Hillary, Krysta, Kenya, Maridel, Megan and Nina; I am grateful and honored by you choosing to dedicate your time to me.

To Tonya Jackman Hampton, EdD, thank you for writing my foreword, I have always respected your wisdom and professional perspective. It is an honor to have you support me.

Finally, to you, the person who decided to use this book. I thank you for dedicating time to do the work—and being a part of making a difference.

I realize the acknowledgments are longer than normal, yet appropriate because if not for all the above experiences and relationships I myself would not have my #perspective.

About the Author

I was proudly raised in "The South," which I say because it has become the proverbial founding teacher of my work, and the basis of who I have become. I am honored to say I'm a daughter, sister, niece, cousin, friend, wife, mother, woman, woman of color, the oldest, a corporate transient, a child of God, a failure, a successor and much more. All of these factors of me make me. It's not only who I am to others that humbly makes me who I am, but the guidance and legacy of my parents are keystones as well. My mother is a dedicated long-standing educator, and my father was one of the first two appointed Black patrol officers in the 1970s in our small county in the South. I express these things for the simple point of clarifying that we are intricate and complex beings. We don't know everything about each other or ourselves in that manner.

The unique thing about me is that I was a very shy child. I was not too fond of any attention towards me, and growing up in a small town—I was not too fond of the fact people could reference who I was. It didn't help that my father would come to the school in his uniform and patrol car. Ironically, since I was young, I have had a passion for people's rights and community service. My desire to make a difference outweighed my fear and comfort of being an introvert. I was a South Carolina State Student Government representative by high school, speaking and presenting workshops about service and teamwork. I was recognized by the South Carolina State Senate my senior year for my contributions to my community and school. It was considered a citizenship award.

I entered Clemson University and continued my resolve for the community. By my senior year, I was nominated and awarded as an Algernon Sydney Sullivan award recipient. I am honored to be among recipients like First Lady Elanor Roosevelt, Fred (Mr.) Rogers, and Supreme Court Justice Lewis Powell. Still, I never thought I was doing enough—I was doing what was needed.

I started my career as a Human Resources Practitioner for Fortune 100 and 500 companies. I loved the experiences in employee relations, labor relations, change management, as well as my leadership opportunities of being part of pioneering national projects within Diversity, Equity, and Inclusion (DEI). I founded my business because I wanted more liberty to speak for transformation and challenging status quos.

I am still continually reflecting, learning, researching, questioning, and defending anything and anyone that is underrepresented. I would always rather be in the background—and my work in the foreground. I never felt like I was in the forefront of the line, yet I was feverishly on the sideline doing my due diligence of service for humanity, relationships and inclusion.

I write this book for those who are scared to be on the front lines—the ones who believe that to be an ally or advocate, you must look or act a certain way. If you are willing to be vulnerable, do the work, and take a step, you are one step further than before.

The world needs you to do more. You are a vital link to making this world better by helping people feel like they belong.

If a quiet, scared small-town girl who used to hide behind her father could learn to live in several places across the United States and find her voice to make a difference, I know if you bring the effort with this guided journal, you can step out more courageously than you ever have before.

Kendra Q. Dodd is Founder and Principal consultant for Fulfil-2B, LLC, a consulting and coaching firm.

Foreword

It takes courage to assert oneself in a working or social environment that fails to extend to you a feeling of inclusion. After two years of social distancing and periods of isolation, the timing is perfect for Kendra Dodd to release her book, *Perspectives*, which introduces new ways for us to learn about ourselves and others. The book gives us the tools to use this information and make a positive impact in our environment.

Dodd reminds us that it is human nature to want to be included and to belong. She shows us how persistent self-examination can help guide us toward more inclusion, and a greater sense of belonging. This is especially important for a world on the backside of the world's most challenging and fearful point of exclusion – the global Coronavirus pandemic.

In *Perspectives*, the author acknowledges that facing fear is a fundamental part of moving toward appreciating self and gaining growth. She shows readers how being intentional and crossing bridges are necessary steps toward making an impact in that growth. The book *Perspectives* as a way for individuals to intentionally learn essential aspects of their selves through many reflective, thought-provoking questions.

Perspectives offers readers an opportunity to reflect and respond to questions through journaling, which teaches us that our active intentions can lead to infinite bridges, making a powerful impact for ourselves and the people and processes around us.

Dodd is committed to helping us make a transformative change, which happens when we're willing to reflect. Throughout this book, outlines questions and exercises to guide reflection. She also shows us how to have multiple bridge moments in order to experience transformational change naturally. Bridge moments take us to the next phase of those changes in our lives. In *Perspectives*, she challenges us to self-develop and recognize the mission of accepting how we can benefit from including, belonging and embracing differences. The acceptance alone is the bridge moment.

The author encourages readers to strive for bridge moments without expecting perfection, but rather to work toward growth. *Perspectives* is intriguing and inspirational. The book affirms it is necessary to be vulnerable in order to grow and transform. In its many pages, *Perspectives* establishes that our transformation is necessary for growth of others and to make an impact in the world.

The encouragement she embeds in her book for readers is remarkable. Her work illustrates that we all have the capacity to be leaders as a result of our own self-analysis. Readers are encouraged by the thought provoking questions.

One of my favorite topics is the values list. Dodd provides a list of values and allows readers to add a few of their own. Another fascinating section is about our great fears. These, along with the other important areas of self-reflection, are keys to reaching a better understanding of inclusion and belonging. She also beautifully elevates many quotes and the work of other authors, which augment the development and reflection questions and exercises offered to readers. The author encourages her readers along the way with congratulatory remarks and ways to build bridges to deeper self-awareness and relationships with others.

Dodd's *SEED* method is on point! It helps us see how we view differences, and helps us make better decisions when we apply it. The application of the *SEED* method leads to improving our leadership skills in the workplace.

Take your time with the book. It is an artful, non-linear invitation to learn about yourself. So – Jump In! Kendra Dodd does an outstanding job creating a space for you to do so.

~Tonya Jackman Hampton, EdD
Chief People and Culture Officer – Hennepin Healthcare
Founder and Chief Advisor – Sequel Consulting Group, LLC

Table of Contents

Why I Wrote This Book

"If nothing changes, nothing changes."

This anonymous quotation is one of my favorites. Why? Because it is a relentless reminder that if there is any dissatisfaction with one's current state, some form of change must occur.

Many people complain and say they want to see change. We have all heard people complain about work, relationships, kids, their boss, the government, school, teachers, students, neighbors, colleagues, clients, or just their overall life. The complaints are usually focused on what others need to do to make the situation better, not realizing we each should include ourselves in the equation *if we really want to see change.* It's easier to believe that change must happen externally only. I am as guilty and human as anyone in succumbing to this fallacy.

The best influencers are the ones that "walk the talk." We are all influencers—leaders of our actions and reactions. We all play a role, and are responsible for the culture and environment in which we dwell.

Almost without fail, when I enter into a relationship with a client, they have a list of to-dos and tasks to accomplish. They are energized and state, "I want to learn and change now. I'm ready!" After reviewing and discussing their exhaustive list and the timeline, they usually expect results immediately.

It is easy to create a list and use it as proof of readiness. Creating lists or completing items on a list, does not represent proof of change or improvement. It just proves that one has adequate task management skills.

Before accepting a client, the critical question I ask is: "What is the one thing that you want to accomplish? What is your number one priority?" Often, these questions can cause paralysis because it's easier to throw out a list of desires without really spending time on the main root purpose for wanting to change. Once they answer the above, the next question is, "Why is *that* the priority?"

Change can be simple; change can be quick and often externally orientated. Making a statement, creating a policy, and implementing a process is change. Re-doing your wardrobe is change. A true transformation or transition is a growth process. It's a psychological process to make sense or come to terms with change. Transition and transformation cannot be managed by others, it is all internal. People rarely can go cold turkey and change. They "change" in small increments, aka, transformational change.

Do you have a desire for a lasting difference? Lasting change will take longer than a few hours of training or enlightenment on a topic. Sustainable change will require the genuine need for cultural evolution. To experience true transformation, it must start with the heart of internal intention.

When I first got married, a good friend gave us a set of books on marriage. One book was for the husband, and one was for the wife. Each was specifically written and designed to help each person become a better partner. It provided direction on things we each needed to do and accomplish to be better spouses. I loved the book so much that I started giving this set to couples as wedding gifts. One of those couples decided they didn't like what was written for them and stopped reading their book—and instead started reading the other's book—and then started holding their spouse accountable for the things in their book. This is an obvious example of how we can expect change but miss the fact that actual progress won't happen *if we don't change ourselves.* Remember, if nothing changes, nothing changes.

As a consultant and coach, I receive numerous requests to help leaders, teams, and their individual members embrace change and progress to a growth mindset culture. They want to become more inclusive, create a place of belonging, embrace differences, and understand equity concepts. Unfortunately, the timeframe or capacity for longer-lasting transformation becomes challenging. That is how the idea of this guided journal began.

I wanted to create an environment where deep and intentional work is done. When people say, "do the work," this guided journal contains the type of work that should be done. Uncomfortable self-reflection leads to real progress; growth happens outside your comfort zone. If you want to be a change agent, it must start with you. You must embark on your journey.

Being educated does not automatically make a person better; reading to obtain knowledge is just improving your intellect. The ability to integrate your emotional meaning, reconsider and analyze your behavior with what you learn, is transformation. This book will guide you to do that kind of work.

Expecting change without a full assessment is temporarily compelling, yet long-term it is unproductive. It is hypocrisy to criticize others for their faults, and tell them to improve—if you are unwilling to do the same for yourself. This book is meant to help you reflect on how you can be part of the change.

Introduction

Welcome!

You are about to embark on an exploration to learn more about yourself and others. I am incredibly excited that you have decided to take this journey.

The goal is to help slow down your knee-jerk reactions, to help you understand others and apply empathy. It will also help you appreciate and understand that you can make a difference and identify when you are distracted by fear and the triggers that are causing discourse. The book's design helps you spend a substantial amount of intentional work building relationships, self-confidence, conversations, and collaborations that yield sustainable transformation toward an improved culture that you will embody.

Guided Journal Companion Options

- **Consecutive Days**

If you decide to dedicate a few minutes a day, this will yield the highest transformation because you will be improving day by day. Each entry, on average, should not take you longer than six to nine minutes total in the beginning. As time progresses, it can take longer because some assignment challenges require more responses, and more self-reflection. Those assignments can take up to one-hour maximum. (Note: this will not be the norm.)

- **Precisely Timed Schedule (Clustering)**

I realize life happens, and you might not be able to commit to entries daily. I would recommend setting a specific goal. The clearer your purpose, the higher probability it will be accomplished. When do you plan to complete the guided journal? Then break it down into how many entries need to be completed in that time frame.

For example, if you have a six-month goal, that is an average of almost 19 entries a month, or a little over four entries a week, Essentially, it gives you weekends off, with a couple of free bonus days that month.

- **Individual or Partners**

You can move through this guided journal on your own. The concept is a personal and individual voyage. It is specially designed to be processed by only you. You can successfully reach transformation alone.

But I would recommend having an accountability partner to keep you on task to complete the guided journal. The primary purpose would be to support completion, but at your comfort level, you can arrange meeting times to share your overviews and highlights.

- **Groups**

This book can be an excellent resource for teams, book clubs, departments, or even organizations. The purpose is not to confidentially share your entries, but rather to create visions, missions, and tactics of how key revelations can help you to lead and to "show up" differently than before. Discussions will be on culture progression and individual responsibility with a goal to help build a better culture. If the decision is to utilize groups, I would highly recommend appointing a facilitator. Having an identified person will help assure the group discussion is appropriately guided and managed, and that participants will be provided the opportunity to contribute. *Disclaimer:* I am not a clinically licensed practitioner and do not claim to be. If at any time during this journey the experience causes a response that is uncomfortably difficult for you, I highly recommend speaking with a professional to navigate your emotions further.

"Your" Guided Journal

A guide is a person who advises or shows the way to others. A guide will lead people through experiences on a journey. This book will help you traverse several bridges.

The symbolism of a bridge works here because a bridge provides passage over a complicated obstacle. A bridge does not eliminate the obstacle, but rather provides a way to overcome it.

One of the reasons this guided journal was created was to help people reflect on themselves, identify the obstacle, and move beyond fear. One of the most prevalent reasons that people are hindered from moving forward is fear.

What are these fears?

- The fear of saying and doing the wrong thing.
- The complexity of determining where and how you fit into change.
- Worrying about speaking up. What do you say?
- Feeling triggered by anger or experiencing sensitivity regarding a topic?

The bridge is where you steer, build, and overcome. Bridge-building can be uncomfortable, yet if you continue, it can be the means to success in your progressive journey.

How will this book help you be better? You will improve your understanding of :

1) the source of your fears and anxieties
2) how to be empathetic of other's journeys, and

3) how to be the bridge for others to feel safe in the journey with you.

Where do you start?

It starts before the bridge.

A bridge can be traversed two ways. You can cross it one way to reach a destination, and you have the ability to return. For example, suppose a person continually talks over you and others. In that case, the first time you speak up will be challenging, if not scary. Yet if this situation occurs again, you are now experienced, and addressing the problem the next time shouldn't be as concerning as the first time.

A bridge doesn't destroy what is behind you; it becomes a passageway for future use.

Each time you encounter a disagreement with someone, or a difference of opinion, or feel like you are not recognized, respected, or valued you are encountering what I call a "bridge moment." A bridge moment is when you are facing a disconnect with the other person. Bridge moments or disagreements can occur daily. What do you do when you encounter this "bridge moment"? What choice do you usually make when you disagree with someone? Do you make the choice to cross the bridge— meaning you say something, or do you decide to not say anything—and stay in the "land of intentions"?

As you take your journey, you will collect badges of accomplishment to help you celebrate milestones. After this book, you will have a certificate of completion. The dedicated time you spend should be honored, celebrated, and recognized.

This progressive journey and learning is segmented into three stages:

1) The Intentions Component—*your current state, present mindset, and experience.*
2) The Bridge Component—*the questioning, the discovery, and the challenge of status quo or current perception.*
3) The Impact Component—*the outcome of the paradigm perspective and change.*

Stage I: Intentions

*"People with good intentions but limited understanding are more
dangerous than people with total ill will."*
~Martin Luther King Jr.

The intention stage is often dismissed and rejected for two reasons:

- It is not valued because it is perceived as time-consuming or a waste of time or not action-oriented enough. Other times there is resentment and unresolved emotions and feelings within this stage. Therefore, it can be challenging for people to process.
- This stage also includes personal ownership and accountability that some find difficult to accept.

If this stage is not effectively processed, the same patterns of issues and obstacles will continue to arise in your life.

Why do you want to change in the first place? What are your intentions or motivations for taking the steps toward thinking or acting differently?

The evaluation of your intentions should be done first before crossing the bridge.

Exploring intentions is not the same as setting actions or setting goals. Setting intentions is spending time understanding the heart, the why, determining what you believe, discovering where the belief comes from, and clarifying your values. I am a fan of vision and goals, but the common problem I see is that goals are not set correctly. Goals are sometimes quickly set as action-based tasks without a true vision or reason for having the goal in first place. Often, people are really setting actions—and not goals. A true goal answers the question: Why am I doing this?

Repeatedly, I have seen individuals, groups, and corporations immediately create measures, plans, and tactics without spending valuable time reflecting on the current state, future vision, and purpose for tackling the task in the first place. Stating "it's the right thing to do" is not enough. You must know why you believe the task is the correct course of action.

The mission that we are focusing on with this book is inclusion, belonging, embracing differences, and the plight for equity—learning how to advocate in your space.

To set an intention is to align heart and mind to strategic action. The purpose is to assess values and instill meaning behind thoughts and then actions.

Foundational Pillars of Intentions

Stage One is a critical section of the book. It is the foundation to help you navigate through the remainder of the book. The quote from Martin Luther King Jr. is profound with regard to why this portion of the book is so relevant. When someone is not aware of how they are impacting someone, and not understanding the root of the behaviors, they will repeatedly but unintentionally hurt others, limit their relationships, and damage even potential trust. At least a person who is intentionally hurting someone is in control and aware of what they are doing. A person who is not self-aware is essentially reckless.

Not only does self-awareness help others, it ultimately benefits you. Research states the more self-aware we are, the more confident, courageous, and creative we are. Our decisions are better, and we have the ability to communicate more effectively. This discussion is vital because studies reveal that only 10–15 percent of people are self-aware. The studies also show that the higher your role of leadership, the more challenging it is to be truly self-aware. Introspection is not self-awareness; self-awareness means that you examine the causes of your thoughts, feelings, and behaviors.

"Self-awareness isn't one truth. It's a delicate balance of two distinct, even competing viewpoints."
~Tasha Eurich, PhD

There are three "Pillars," or fundamental theories, that support this stage. Pillars, in this context, are considered the underlying support to a person's intentions.

The three pillars are:
1) Purpose: *This pillar is a person's genuine desire or logic.*
2) Reflection: *This pillar will help process your beliefs and feelings.*
3) Experience: *This pillar defines the things that have happened to you. It describes your responses and examines the consequence of the reaction.*

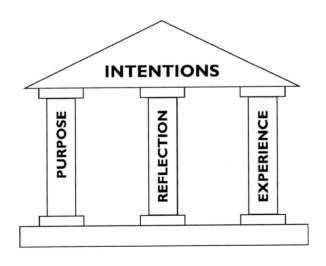

When a company reached out to me to coach one of their employees, they provided my new potential client's background. When I reviewed her demographics, I was confident that the amount of time it would take to assist her with gaining some self-awareness would be very straightforward.

I was wrong; it was quite the opposite!

- She had a very low assessment of herself.
- She did not understand how her behavior was negatively impacting her engagements.
- Initially, she was relentless in feeling it was not her but others.
- She thought that she was not the issue; she blamed jealousy, prejudgments of others, poor leadership, and even discrimination for her work conflicts.
- After several sessions of self-awareness, she recognized the origins of some of her thought processes, which in turn helped her realize that others didn't see things exactly the way she did.
- Her inability to see herself in the equation of the conflict was causing her to be unable to open her perspective and be empathetic to her teammates and manager.

The client did eventually transform with a broader perspective. How did she transform? She did it through a series of exercises like you will do with your guided journal entries. Also, I saw her mindset shift. She had more of a curious disposition, and additionally, she defined her experience, wanting to know others' perception, not just her own. She became less defensive and more inquisitive. Lastly, she was honest and authentic with her true feelings regarding situations.

This section will be as enjoyable as you allow it to be—therefore, let it be a positive journey for you.

Lastly, the more you understand yourself, the easier it is to help others understand you. I will help you in that endeavor. This is a beautiful view and experience if you allow it.

Pillar 1: Purpose

"We must have a theme, a goal, a purpose in our lives. If you don't know where you're aiming, you don't have a goal."
~Mary Kay Ash

- Purpose—it's the reason for which something is done or exists. You will explore your intention and the defined meaning in this guided journal for you.
- You will establish the plan or the aim for accomplishment. There are five assignments under this pillar. These exercises will help clarify the reasons and objectives of your journey.

Your Purpose of Intent

"The road to hell is paved with good intentions."
~Henry G. Bohn

The word *intention* can have so many idioms, definitions, and interpretations. Intentions can be our scapegoat and, at the same time, be our driving force to change.

When we say we are going to do something, we don't always do it. The excuse used is that we "intended" to do it. It becomes the ideal of the intention to change, but we don't. The choices to keep the New Year's resolution, the will to read that book, the intention to call someone back, the intention to exercise or eat better, and in the end, we do not do any of it. All are expressed with intent, yet are never executed.

Then there are the times the word *intention* is used, and things are completed. The intention is to set a goal, and the goal is established and accomplished.

What are your intentions with this book?

- To think about change?
- To be excited about the idea of changing?
- To be convinced to change?
- To say you got the book to prove you are trying to learn or develop?

What are your true intentions? Really? What are your plans for what you learn here? What is your hope and desire for change? What difference do you want the knowledge to make in your life?

Activity/Assignment:
Think about...

1) a time when you successfully accomplished your intentions

2) a time you barely completed them

3) a time where you didn't achieve them at all

What was different about each situation? Were your actions different? If so, how? Write your response below.

One key difference is the truth. Your truth. Intention can just be a thought, or intention can mean a genuine desire and purpose. Understanding your truth is imperative.

> *"This above all; To thine own self be true."*
> ~William Shakespeare

Ask yourself:

What is your "truth" regarding this exercise?

What do you want to accomplish when you finish?

What are you willing to do?

Are you ready to fully complete the activities and assignments?

Understanding your true intentions will lead to better satisfaction, experience, and success. State your clear objective. For example, will you commit to answering all questions and genuinely reflect to help make sure you are applying the learning?

Overcoming Ambivalence

"Ambivalence is like carbon monoxide—undetectable yet deadly."
~Cherie Carter-Scott

Ambivalence is the crossroads to growth. It is the place where the ideals of intention are or are not acted upon.

You may have the lingering subconscious question—will the effort of reading and completing the entries in this guided journal be worth it? There still could be conflicting feelings about dedicating the time to being more conscious of your thoughts and behaviors. The purpose of this book is not to be enlightened by thoughts, ideas, or concepts but to be more attuned to your behavior, looking at the differences of others' behaviors, and showing up differently because of it. You may be thinking "let's just see." "Waiting to see" is the hallmark of ambivalence; there is no commitment.

Have you ever worked with someone who worked on a project but you could tell they were not fully invested? Don't be like them. Don't be lukewarm. Decide you will commit to some form of change.

Are you truly willing to devote to bettering your having a heart and mind?

There may be a part of you that recognizes the importance of learning other perspectives. Then there may be part of you that asks, how much do I have to change? Will you be giving something up to change? You may be saying; I am happy the way I am and what I believe. The angst of the unknown is normal. It's human. Also, your mind is very intuitive. If you do not clearly lay out what you will do, you will not commit to anything. Behaviors will divert to what it knows, which is your current state of thought.

Activity/Assignment:
Today, I want you to process how you feel about yourself and other perspectives. What are you willing to consider? What are you *not* ready to think about or discuss? Answer the questions below.

What are your negotiables? What are you willing to consider related to expanding your mindset? Think about things you don't know enough about to have an opinion and/or experience? Are you ready to learn more about it? Examples could be immigration, first-generation students, or simple things like whether pineapple should be on pizza.

What are your non-negotiables? What are the things that are the foundation of who you are and what you believe? What are things that you are not willing at all to examine? Examples could include specific theology, abortion, or discussions of should women pay when on a date?

What is it about this book that gives you apprehension? For example, are you are not sure if you will feel comfortable speaking up on things after reading the book?

What are you sure of? What about this journey interests you? What is exciting to think about in completing the exercises? For example, are you interested in self-reflecting on what is important that you learn to speak up about?

You are not being graded or judged. There is not a right or a wrong way to use this journal. You are at liberty to determine how much you would like to progress. If you decide just to be enlightened, so be it. What person likes to be told what to do? So, what do you want to do?

"Wasting time is robbing oneself.
~Estonian Provers

I don't want you to rob yourself of time in doing something that you do not have any plans to truly consider. I am not trying to talk you out of completing this book. On the contrary, I want you to be realistic of what you want to accomplish. The clearer that is—the higher probability you will receive what you expect.

There are enough pressures in life, and I am not trying to add any to you. I want you to find the liberation of choosing your path and making sure you get to your own goal. This journey is for you, yet at the same time, it could positively impact others.

Appreciation

"Knowledge is no value unless you put it into practice."
~Anton Chekhov

The word appreciation is defined and used in many ways. The Latin origin is the word *appreciate*, meaning to set a price or appraise. In the financial world, financial appreciation refers to the increase in value of an asset over time.

This experience could yield a return on investment (ROI) that could inevitably improve your relationships at home, work, socially, and even personally for you.

Activity/Assignment:
How can this journey be invaluable to you? How can it be an asset? Think of a time where cross-cultural differences have hindered time, productivity, relationships, work, and overall achievement.

If you were more culturally aware, how could this have helped you with prior conflicts? How can this be valuable for you if you sincerely lean in with these assignments?

Prioritizing

"The key is taking responsibility and initiative, deciding what your life is about and prioritizing your life around the most important things."
~Stephen Covey

Sometimes we take on more than we should. We make some things more important than they should be. This makes us say yes to things we should turn down. Honestly, this issue is the story of my life. Do you have this problem? Do you take on more than you should? Do you commit to too much?

I want this time to be challenging yet realistic. One of the main reasons people don't reach their goals is that they don't make them reasonable or specific enough, and the task is too big to be achieved effectively. Please keep it simple.

Ask yourself:

What is the one thing that you want to achieve—the one thing you want to be better at after reading and conducting the exercises?

What is your over-arching goal and accomplishment?

Do you want to better examine your reactions to people when they say or do things differently?

Do you want to improve with your often knee-jerk reaction to take personal offense when someone disagrees with your perspective?

Do you want to be less judgmental and learn how people can see things differently?

What is the most important thing you want to accomplish in the end?

That's what this book is designed to clarify for you.

Activity/Assignment:

Brain dumping is a technique that involves decluttering your mind from lingering thoughts or things you are overthinking—and by doing this, it will help you gain focus. The concept is that by physically placing your thoughts in writing, it tricks the brain into thinking you are doing something about the thoughts (which you are).

This exercise is designed to help free up mental stress, clear the mind, and help you organize your thoughts.

I want you to complete a brain-dumping exercise. Complete the following steps below.

Step 1: Express all the things you would like to gain after reading this book. There are no right or wrong answers. Write them all out below. *(Note: You can review the past entries from prior assignments)*
Step 2: Circle your top five-to-ten goals from your list.
Step 3: Out of the five to ten circled, place a star next to your top three in that list.

_____   _____

_____   _____

_____   _____

_____   _____

_____   _____

_____   _____

_____   _____

_____   _____

_____   _____

Step 4: Out of the top three-starred, which one would yield the highest return? Which one would improve your life the most?

The final response will be your number one goal for this journey. Re-write your number-one priority below.

Making a Promise – Taking the Pledge

*"Unless a commitment is made, there are only promises
and hopes, but no plans."*
~Peter Drucker

Taking a pledge is a psychological strategy for sticking to a goal. The idea of writing and signing a pledge is a pre-commitment that now goes beyond stating intentions. It becomes a promise—a promise to be true to something you believe.

Another way to increase the success of a commitment is to work with someone, have a partner(s) to hold you accountable, and make it enjoyable.

I recommend sharing this journey with at least one person and having them sign the pledge with you. Having a dependable person aware of your goal can help you stay on track, and non-judgmentally encourage and support you.

Activity/Assignment:
Complete the Promise Card below. Identify an accountability partner and have them sign an agreement as well or write their name if they are not in the same physical space as you.

You've got this! I have faith that you will fulfill the promise you have for yourself. Well wishes and cheers for you as you dive into the journey.

My Promise

I _____ *(your name)* **will commit to**

_____ *(your priority)*

by _____ *(specific actions).*

I will follow-up with _____ *(accountability*

partner name) _____ *(frequency of updates)* **to let them**

know how I am doing with my commitment.

If I become challenged in accomplishing my promise I will

_____ *(action that will be taken).*

_____

(your signature)

_____

(date)

_____

(accountability partner signature, if applicable)

_____

(date)

Pillar 2: Reflection

"Sometimes, you have to look back in order to understand the things that lie ahead."
~Yvonne Woon

Congratulations! You officially have a clear path of how you will utilize this book. Welcome to Pillar Two of the Intentions Stage.

This section will examine your emotions, feelings, and beliefs on various ethics and values. It will help you formally clarify your core values. This is important because they affect the decisions you make and the responses you exhibit.

Joy

"If you carry joy in your heart, you can heal any moment."
~Carlos Santana

Reflection:

What makes you happy?

What naturally makes you smile with joy?

How do you feel when you are your happiest self?

When are you at most peace?

The Utmost

*"The most important thing in life is knowing
the most important things in life."*
~David F. Jakielo

Reflection:

What matters most to you?

What are the most important things you are not willing to give up—and
will fight for in your life?

What are your negotiables? What are you willing to compromise?

Have you ever compromised your non-negotiables? If so, what happened.
What do you think was the reason for the compromise?

Love

"I'm not a smart man.
But I know what love is."
~Forrest Gump

Reflection:

What is love? How would you describe or define love? Do you believe there are different kinds of love? If so, what are they?

What are some examples and expressions of love?

How do you show expressions of love?

What do you believe are never expressions of love? Is love important for society? Why or why not?

Respect

"Mutual respect is the foundation
of genuine harmony."
~Dalai Lama

Reflection:
How would you define respect?

What does respect look like to you? Give specific behaviors and examples about your experiences of respect.

What are verbal signs of respect? What are non-verbal signs of respect?

Are respect and love the same? Can you love someone and not show respect? What is considered disrespect? Provide examples of what that looks like to you.

What is the ultimate form of disrespect to you?

Annoyance

"Annoyance is a physical malady that is in no way cured just because the annoying situation that causes it is eliminated."
~Friedrich Nietzsche

Reflection:

What are your pet peeves? What are things that you particularly find annoying? What actions, words, nuisances, and behaviors do you find completely unacceptable, yet they may seem small or insignificant to others?

Why do you feel this way about this irritant?

Examples: chewing loudly, people being late, people who interrupt when someone is talking, misspelling or using incorrect grammar on social media, PDA (public displays of affection)

Pet Peeve	Reason for Annoyance	Usually by Whom?

Do you believe your pet peeves are justified? Why or why not?

Truths

"Wisdom is found only in truth."
~Von Goethe

Reflection:

What are inevitable or non-argumentative truths? What makes something the truth? What makes it a principle and a doctrine?

Can truth ever be questioned? How can one person's truth be different from another person's truth? Is truth objective, relative or subjective?

What does "finding truth" mean? Can you find the truth? How is truth recognized?

Is truth important in your life? Why?

Untruths

Reflection:
What is a lie? How would you define lying? How do you feel about lying?

Is there ever a time lying can be justified? Do you believe in a white lie? Is lying morally wrong? Is it normal to lie? Can lying ever be good?

Have you ever lied? Why? If so, who has it usually been with? For example, *authority figure, loved one, stranger.*

Do you hold others who lie with equal contempt as you would yourself?

Write your response in the columns below:

Situation	Yes/No	Why?
Have you ever pretended? For example, pretending to like something that you didn't, yet pretended you did to make that person feel better?		
Have you ever withheld a disagreement to avoid conflict?		
Have you ever positioned something on social media to embellish a situation?		

Would you consider any of these circumstances lies? If so, which ones?

Are there lies that you feel you even tell yourself? (i.e., Imposter Syndrome, which is doubting your abilities and feeling like a fraud).

Disagreements and Discord

"Out of clutter, find simplicity. From discord, find harmony.
In the middle of difficulty lies opportunity."
~Albert Einstein

Reflection:
Are conflicts bad? Why? Are conflicts good? If so, When?

Have you ever avoided a conflict?

Do you ever feel comfortable addressing a conflict? What would make you comfortable enough for it to be addressed?

Do you feel uncomfortable disagreeing with others?

Are there certain people you have more of a challenge disagreeing with?

Forgiving

Reflection:

Do you find it hard to forgive? Why?

Are there things that are unforgivable to you? What or who is easier to forgive?

Does a person have to do or say something before you forgive them? What would a person have to do for you to forgive them?

Have you ever apologized and asked for forgiveness, and it was not accepted? How did it make you feel? Does that still affect you?

Trust

"Trust is the glue of life. It's the most essential ingredient in effective communication. It's the foundational principle that holds all relationships."
~ Stephen Covey

Reflection:
How is trust gained for you? What actions and events must occur to gain your trust?

Do you believe that you must gain the trust of others? Do you think that people should automatically trust you? What actions or things do you do to gain trust from others?

What can cause you to lose trust with someone?

What causes you to mistrust someone? What actions do they possess/demonstrate?

What would it take for a person to gain your trust back if it is lost?

Are there certain people you trust more than others? Why or why not?

Are there certain people you distrust less than others? Why or why not?

Values

"If you don't stick to your values when they are being tested,
they are not values, they are hobbies."

~Anonymous

Reflection:

Below is a list of values.

Step 1: Circle all the values you feel represent you and your beliefs. If some are missing, you can write them on the blank lines provided.

Values Exercise:

Abundance	Dependability	Knowledge	Professionalism
Acceptance	Discipline	Leadership	Public Service
Accountability	Diversity	Learning	Punctuality
Achievement	Empathy	Love	Recognition
Advancement	Empowerment	Loyalty	Reputation
Affection	Encouragement	Making a Difference	Restoration
Adventure	Energy	Maturity	Relationships
Advocacy	Enthusiasm	Meaningful Work	Religion
Ambition	Environmental	Ministry	Reliability
Appreciation	Equality	Mindfulness	Resilience
Attractiveness	Ethics	Motivation	Be Role Model
Autonomy	Excellence	Optimism	Resourcefulness
Balance	Expressiveness	Open-Mindedness	Responsibility
Beauty	Experimentation	Originality	Responsiveness

Being the Best	Fairness	Order	Self-Control
Benevolence	Family	Patience	Serenity
Boldness	Fitness	Partnership	Simplicity
Calmness	Friendship	Passion	Stability
Caring	Flexibility	Performance	Status
Challenge	Forgiveness	Personal Development	Supportive
Charity	Forward-Looking	Proactive	Sustainability
Cheerfulness	Freedom	Professionalism	Straightforward
Clean	Fun	Protection	Success
Cleverness	Generosity	Quality	Teamwork
Community	Grace	Risk-Taking	Thankfulness
Communication	Growth	Safety	Tradition
Commitment	Flexibility	Security	Transformation
Compassion	Happiness	Service	Trustworthiness
Competition	Health	Sincerity	Truth
Consciousness	Honesty	Spirituality	Understanding
Control	Humility	Spontaneity	Uniqueness
Courageousness	Humor	Stability	Usefulness
Cooperation	Inclusiveness	Strategy	Versatility
Collaboration	Independence	Peace	Victory
Consistency	Individuality	Perfection	Vision
Contribution	Innovation	Playfulness	Warmth
Creativity		Pleasure	Wealth
Credibility	Inspiration	Power	Well-Being
Curiosity	Intelligence	Preparedness	Wisdom

Daring	Intuition	Proactivity	Zeal
Decisiveness	Joy	Purpose	_____
Dedication	Kindness	Politics	_____

Step 2: Write your top three-to-five values on the lines below.

Step 3: Define why you chose your top values. Define what that means to you.

Gratefulness

Being grateful is the bridge between the world of nightmares and the world where we are free to say no. It's the bridge between the world of delusions and the world of creativity. It's the power that brings death back to life, the power that turns poverty to wealth and anger to compassion.

~James Altucher

Reflection:

What are you grateful for?

What do you appreciate most about your life?

What experiences are you glad you faced? Why are you grateful for them?

Is it hard for you to be grateful? If so, why?

Do you struggle with being thankful for specific events in your life? If so, what are they?

Are there people that you are glad to have in your life? Who are they, and why?

Do you express your gratitude to others?

Distress

'For it's our grief that gives us our gratitude, Shows us how to find hope,
if we ever lose it. So ensure that this ache wasn't endured in vain:
Do not ignore the pain. Give it purpose. Use it.

~Amanda Gorman

Reflection:

Distress is considered unhealthy stress. Is there some distress that has been hard for you to overcome?

What is your greatest fear?

What increases your fear? What lessens your fear?

Are most of your fears experience-derived or mentally provoked?

How do you respond to your fear? Are your responses to fear manageable?

Do you recognize the beginning stages of fear for you? How does your body respond to fear?

Do you have any phobias? Where do you think they come from? Are any of your phobias unintentional and unconscious?

Do you believe fear is natural? If so, how? In what ways can fear be unhealthy?

What fears would you like to release?

Fulfillment

"Your work is going to fill a large part of your life, and the only way to be truly satisfied is to do what we believe is great work. And the only way to do great work is to love what you do."
~Steve Jobs

Reflection:
What makes you proud? What are you most proud of?

Is it hard sharing your achievements with others? If so, why? Do you think it is essential to share your accomplishments with people?

Are there certain people or situations where you find it more challenging to share your attributes and talents?

Are there times when it is not appropriate to show your talents?

What's something about your own ethnic/cultural group that makes you proud? Nationality? Gender? Etc.

Coping

"It's not the load that breaks you down, it's the way you carry it."
~Lou Holtz

Reflection:
How do you cope? How do you deal with stress?

Do you think you handle pressures well? Are there specific pressures more challenging to manage than others?

Do you self-impose stress? Is it mainly internal or external situations that cause you to stress? What causes you anxiety? Is anxiety different than stress for you? If so, do you manage each differently?

Have you always coped this way? How is it different? How is it similar?

How do you look for assistance with coping?

What works best for you?

Anger

"Not being outraged by anything is a superpower."
~James Pierce

Reflection:
What makes you angry?

Is it normal to be angry? Is being angry healthy? Is there ever a time it is unhealthy?

Do you usually apologize if you have potentially crossed the line with your anger? Why or why not?

Do you think a person can be provoked to anger?

"Anger is an acid that can do more harm to the vessel in which it is stored than to anything on which it is poured."
~Mark Twain

Have you heard that anger is a secondary emotion, and is not the first emotion that you feel when a situation arises? If this theory is true—what is usually the first feeling that precedes your anger?

TIME-OUT...PAUSE

Let's take a time-out to review before we move forward. You have done very well.

Many different types of emotions influence how we live and interact with others.

There are several theories about the impact or foundation of emotions. Some theories say there are two or three, and even up to six, basic emotions that a person may have. Then there are theories that say our emotions are hierarchical or that we have primary emotions. Our emotions will produce responses under the guise of whatever feeling we are experiencing.

Emotions can be combined to form different feelings. For example, joy and trust combined can equal love. One thing is for sure; feelings can be complex to explain.

Emotions are linked and understood to be part of health by some cultures. They have also been linked to the physical consequence of a person, from sickness to wellness to even life expectancy. What does the topic of emotion have to do with this book? Emotions can be the essence of who we are and how we show up. Emotions can be a person's identity and how they behave and interact, yet not necessarily equal in reaction. Fear can cause some to be immobilized, while it can cause excitement in others. For example, if three people are talking and one person raised their voice, this may cause one participant to shut down their communication, while at the same time exciting the other to raise their own voice in response.

Emotions play a critical role in our lives that affect our decisions, choices, and behaviors. No feeling is an island unto itself; it is interwoven in the fabric of our lives. Therefore, it can be the main contributor to our perspectives on things.

Activity/Assignment:

Let's pause and reflect on all the emotions of your guided journal entries thus far. Below are all the emotions that you reflected on in Pillar 2: Reflection; follow the steps.

- Step One: Circle the emotion that you manage well.
- Step Two: Place an asterisk next to the emotion you would like to improve or one you don't manage as well as you wish.

Joy   Forgiving
Utmost   Trust
Love   Values
Respect   Gratefulness
Annoyance   Distress
Truths   Fulfillment
Untruths   Coping
Disagreements and Discord   Anger

What do you believe is the reason you manage some emotions better than others? How do you think it is influenced? Do you think it's your personality, how you were raised, the environment?

Pillar 3: Experiences

"Experience is not what happens to you;
it's what you do with what happens to you."
~Aldous Huxley

Experiences are not singular events. They are an evolution or sequence of events. When you experience something, you respond, and that response yields another experience. Then that experience produces another experience, and so on. Our experiences are all compounded from one activity to another.

The only way to potentially change the trajectory of a sequence of experiences is to change the pattern of the reaction.

We will now intentionally study a little more in-depth how our values align with our experience.

Encounters and Relationships

"None of us got where we are solely by pulling ourselves up by our bootstraps."
~Thurgood Marshall

Reflection:

How we view the world has a lot to do with the people we encounter and our relationships. Our success in our challenges is connected to our interaction with a person or group of people. From our intimate family circle to our first group of friends, to the influencers—all of these, and the quality of those relationships, affect our life.

Activity/Assignment:

Select one or two key people in each segment of your life. Describe in detail how they influenced you.

STAGE	KEY INFLUENCER #1	KEY INFLUENCER #2
Childhood		
Pre-teen		
Teen		
Early Adulthood		
Now		

Which relationships still exist? Why or why not? What themes would you say shaped you and your perspective? What essential negative experiences did you have? What key positive experiences?

How has the above affected how you feel and act today?

Did you have to manage a lot of change in your life? What are three significant events that you feel shaped how you see things in life?

What was the last significant change you had to encounter? How did you handle it?

Teasing

"I imagine one of the reasons people cling to their hates so stubbornly is because they sense, once hate is gone, they will be forced to deal with the pain."
~James Baldwin

Reflection:

There are very many complexities tied to teasing. Studies and arguments disect meanings and the level of the impact of teasing, which can land on a continuum from playful, to hurtful, to aggressive.

The studies about how teasing is received are just as varied. Some of those studies tend to be underdeveloped because they are culturally subjective, a problem that can be true with any analysis.

Overall, teasing is a human commonality that is experienced in many ways. The behavioral elements range from standard social norms to personal and emotionally individualized elements. The question is: when does being playful transition to hurtful and then aggressive?

Activity/Assignment:

How do you feel about teasing? Is it okay to tease?

Do you believe there is a healthy form of teasing? If so, how and what are some examples?

What could make teasing healthy or unhealthy?

Are there subjects or topics that should never be teased or joked about? If so, what are they?

Bully: a person who habitually seeks to harm or intimidate those whom they perceive as vulnerable.

Have you ever been bullied? What was the bully like?

Were you ever the bully? If so, why?

How does being a bully impact you today?

Guidance and Influence

"Each person must live their life as a model for others."
~Rosa Parks

Reflection:

People's behavior, especially those in influencing positions or status, can affect the belief and behavior of another person. At impressionable times, especially from childhood to young adult, those "influencer's" guidance could significantly impact a child long-term. Those experiences can directly or indirectly affect relationships, career paths, goals and aspirations for developmental or educational purposes, and even concepts such as financial behavior.

Activity/Assignment:

Seeking counsel. If you were in trouble or had a problem, who would you turn to for advice? Why? What is it about that person that would make you seek their counsel?

How much merit do you give that person? Why? What is that person's strength? Could they ever be wrong? What is it about that person that helps in your growth?

Does the person you seek need to have experience with the topic in which you are seeking advice?

Do you seek several people's counsel before making a decision?

What is the most challenging time in your life? Who was there for you during that time?

If you had a chance to go back to that challenging time—what advice would you tell yourself?

Appreciation and Recognition

"You are not judged by the height you have risen,
but from the depth you have climbed."
~Fredrick Douglas

Reflection:

Recognition helps people understand the value they bring to a person or group. It is an informal or formal way of honoring the contribution of an individual.

Being appreciated means being grateful for that person, to understand their worth and importance to the person, group, or society.

Recognition is more than understanding and appreciating them. It is also showing gratitude to them, an expression which allows the recipient to feel valued.

Several studies show the positive emotional and psychological effects of appreciation, gratitude, and recognition.

Activity/Assignment:

Do you like to be recognized? Why or why not?

How do you like to be appreciated? Do you think it is important to be recognized?

Do you like to be heard? What is most important to you in feeling valued?

Do you feel you have been recognized enough in your life?

Who would you like to be recognized most by?

Who has recognized you the most in your life?

Welcomed

People will forget what you said, people will forget what you did,
but people will never forget how you made them feel.
~Maya Angelou

Reflection:

Welcomed is the positive response to how a person is being treated—
the feeling of being appreciated. Welcomed is associated a lot with the
ideals of hospitality. Welcomed is the response to "I'm glad you are here."

Being welcomed is the happy feeling of being present in the space you
are physically occupying. Feeling welcomed is being comfortable to drop
one's guard.

Activity/Assignment:

Describe an environment where you didn't feel welcome? What about it
didn't feel welcoming?

What was the difference between the environment where you felt welcomed versus where you did not? What were the behaviors of the people?

What kind of environment makes you feel welcome? What about it makes
you feel that way?

Inclusion and Sense of Belonging

"Justice cannot be one side alone,
but must be for both."
~Eleanor Roosevelt

Reflection:

You can be welcomed but still not feel included. Being included has a lot to do with participation and the ability to express yourself with opinions and behaviors.

Inclusion is the response to "I'm glad you are here, and you can share your voice." One step further for inclusion is belonging. *Belonging* is the response to "I value what you have to say, and it is safe to be yourself." Belonging is a higher feeling of connectedness to a particular group.

Inclusion and Belonging foster loyalty and long-lasting relationships.

Activity/Assignment:

Describe a time you felt included. Describe a time where you felt welcomed.

Describe a time where you felt like you truly belonged.

Is there a difference for you between feeling *welcomed* and *included*? If so, how would you describe the difference? What parts are the same for you?

How is your behavior when you feel welcomed and included?

How do people respond to your behavior when you are in those environments? How do you think it is perceived?

Exclusion

"The rights of every man are diminished when the rights of one man are threatened."
~John F. Kennedy

Reflection:

Exclusion is more than not being included. The consequence and the impact of not including someone, and the adverse effects are more sustaining and detrimental. Exclusion has been shown to psychologically increase anxiety, depression, frustration, and loneliness. Exclusion, simply put—is a form of rejection.

Psychologists and social neuroscientists have studied the influence of exclusion regarding our mind, the brain response, and the cause of our behavior.

A person can be excluded physically or emotionally. Physical exclusion is being physically separated, while emotional exclusion is being ignored or being directly told that you are not welcome.

Neuroscientists have proven that similar areas of the brain are activated when we experience physical pain as when we experience social pain. Exclusion is considered social pain. The brain activates and responds the same neurological way to the "pain." It will neurologically function as if you were physically hurt.

The human response can, of course, vary. The reaction could range from being aggressive to passive. It is the simple distinction of *flight, fight or freeze.*

Chronic exclusion effects can be even more traumatic. Chronic exclusion is then the level of intensity or the length of repetitiveness that can play into the long-term negative behaviors.

Activity/Assignment:
Write about a time when you felt left out. Describe the feeling.

How do you react or behave when you feel excluded? Do you become withdrawn, angry, discouraged, etc.? How do you think others perceive your behavior?

Why do you think you respond the way that you do? Do you think your response truly expresses your feelings? Why or why not?

Have you ever been guilty of, or accused of, excluding others? What was the situation? What was your truth? What was your response if accused? Could you relate to their perspective?

TIME-OUT...PAUSE

Time-outs in sports allows the players the ability to reset, strategize and rest. A time-out can help gain perspective and strategically pivot to what's important. It's a small pause before you get back in the game.

It's time for another pause and time-out here. You have covered a lot thus far. Let's review this section before we move forward.

This section concentrated on experiences that are connected to manifesting polarized feelings. Because of the potential intensity, this is an excellent time for a scheduled time to pause in your work.

If you answered the questions and leaned into the experience—you should be immensely proud of yourself! This section may have had you reliving and experiencing the feelings that were warranted or unwanted. If you need a little more time than this pause, take it. If it lingers, I recommend finding a healthy way to process it.

Activity/Assignment:

Let's take a litmus check on how you are currently feeling. Circle the emoji that is closest to how you are presently feeling regarding each category you completed?

Encounters and Relationships	😞 😟 😐 🙂 😊
Teasing	😞 😟 😐 🙂 😊
Guidance and Influence	😞 😟 😐 🙂 😊
Appreciation and Recognition	😞 😟 😐 🙂 😊
Welcomed	😞 😟 😐 🙂 😊
Inclusion and Sense of Belonging	😞 😟 😐 🙂 😊
Exclusion	😞 😟 😐 🙂 😊

In which categories did you have more of a negative feeling? Write down each one and discuss how and what you will do to improve your feeling.

In which categories do you have more of a positive feeling? Write down each one and discuss how you will leverage this positive element.

Transformation

"Things do not change; we change."
~Henry David Thoreau

Reflection:

Personal transformation is a process of changing who you are, and becoming the person you want to be. Human beings have the ability and potential to improve, evolve, and manifest former and current views into new views if they so choose.

As human beings, we can integrate our older, current, and newfound perspective into a transformed and progressed view and consciousness. The best way to describe this is the analogy of the development and strength-building of a muscle. Muscle growth is the result of the complex process of adding stress to the muscle. This stress breaks downs the fibers, and when the muscle repairs itself, it becomes stronger over time. During the process it can be challenging, but in the end you are stronger. The opposite can occur as well, and if you stop adding stress, the muscle isn't as strong and loses strength. It's the same muscle. What changes is the muscle encountering challenges and going through the stress.

Personal transformation follows a similar trajectory. You must constantly challenge your thinking and learning and apply actions to your new insight. If you ever stop challenging yourself, the growth and transformation can stop as well.

Personal change reforms more to external modifications. Coloring our hair, changing our wardrobe, even the change of behavior is all external. Just because a person's outward actions change, it does not accurately mean they have changed internally.

Transformation is the internal modification of a belief. Undoubtedly, the inner transformation will likely produce external change—one is more anecdotal than the other.

Activity/Assignment:

What was the most significant transformation you have experienced in which you used to think at one end of a spectrum on a subject, and now have almost completely changed your view? How did that change occur? How old were you?

What were the outcomes of that changed opinion?

Self-Acceptance

"The truth is: Belonging starts with self-acceptance. Your level of belonging, in fact, can never be greater than your level of self-acceptance, because believing that you're enough is what gives you the courage to be authentic, vulnerable and imperfect."
~Brene Brown

Reflection:

Embrace who you are—the strengths, the weaknesses, the attributes, and the flaws. Accepting ourselves unconditionally is self-acceptance. *Self-acceptance* is simply the ability to be nice to ourselves, and give ourselves grace.

Do you treat yourself better, worse, or the same as you treat others? Our self-acceptance is harmoniously paired with our experiences.

Self-acceptance can be challenging. It is a fallacy to believe that it will result in a positive change if we heavily criticize ourselves. Unhealthy self-acceptance produces anxiety—not the assumed liberation and positive self-esteem we think self-criticizing will do.

Experiences and tendencies in the environment you live in can be the backdrop to encourage unproductive self-acceptance.

The reality is that practicing healthy self-acceptance helps us discover our talents, gifts, and successes within ourselves, and it impacts our relationship with others.

Activity/Assignment:

Complete the form below, determine how you relate to the statement in the left column on a scale of one to ten. Circle the number you identify with the most. If you circle "one," it means you feel least like the statement, while "ten" is you feel most like the statement.

I give myself grace when I make a mistake.	1 2 3 4 5 6 7 8 9 10
When I am criticized, I listen to the feedback and do not take it personally.	1 2 3 4 5 6 7 8 9 10
I am not intimidated by someone more successful than I am. I feel confident that I have attributes I can bring to the relationship.	1 2 3 4 5 6 7 8 9 10
I will express and defend my opinion even when most people's opinions differ from mine.	1 2 3 4 5 6 7 8 9 10
I like and accept myself. This includes my flaws and challenges.	1 2 3 4 5 6 7 8 9 10
When I meet an obstacle, I feel confident that I will overcome it.	1 2 3 4 5 6 7 8 9 10
I don't worry and have no fear of being judged and rejected by other people.	1 2 3 4 5 6 7 8 9 10
When I am dissatisfied with a critical segment or behavior in my life, I will take action steps to make the change.	1 2 3 4 5 6 7 8 9 10

Is there any theme from the assessments above? What are they? Any "aha" moments? Which statement would you like to improve? How?

Responsibility

"Everything depends on upbringing."
~Leo Tolstoy

Reflection:

Being a responsible adult does not begin when you arrive at legal age. Being an accountable _____ *(fill in the blank of your current accountabilities, i.e., parent, sibling, man, woman, leader, citizen, etc.)* does not begin when the title is awarded.

Ironically, some studies show that responsibilities are connected to self-esteem, customs, past role expectations, and accountabilities. Therefore, your concept of accepting responsibilities starts during childhood. The practice and the level of support a child receives plays a large role in how they show up and experience their life. Some psychologists state that the "response" and the allowance of a person to exercise their "abilities" equates to how they will accept and perform in the future. Each stage of life, depending on the accountabilities and the age appropriateness of the expectation, determines how responsibility will be achieved. Other factors include how the commitment was reinforced, rewarded, and accomplished.

Activity/Assignment:

Below write the roles and responsibilities you experienced in your life from past to current. The second column labeled "past" allows room for your thoughts about the topics in the first column during childhood. The third column is for your belief and experience now as an adult. For example, as a child/teen/younger adult, you may have believed that home-schooled children did not have the same social allowances as children who went to school outside of the home. Now, you may think that children can have more social experiences because they can travel and experience life socially more than a child attending school in one place.

Role/ Responsibility of a:	Explain your personal experience and what you witnessed as well.	
	Past	Now
Child/ Adolescence		
Teenager/ Young Adult		
Leader/Elder		
Woman/Man		
Politicians/ Government		
Educators/ Education		

Do you hold some people to a higher expectation than others? Who? Do you believe there should be a higher responsibility for some than others? What are those things? If so, why do you hold them differently?

In the past, when you didn't do things that were expected of you, what were your consequences? Do you think your past plays a factor in your current behavior? Must you be asked to take on responsibility or do you offer to accept a responsibility before being asked?

Your True North

"Our plans miscarry because they have no aim. When a man does not know what harbor he is making for, no wind is the right wind."

~Seneca

Reflection:

True North is considered your inner sense or calling of what life is about, and how you should live and accomplish it. It is a combination of your values, beliefs, and purpose.

True North helps you stay aligned with what is true to you. It will then help you determine which choices, directions, or paths to take. It is your inner compass. Our purpose can evolve from our innate drive and our personal experience.

Activity/Assignment:

What is the driving force in your life? What is the critical core anchor that consistently gives you hope and drives you to be your best?

What do you feel is your purpose in life?

Teamwork: Compromising and Collaboration

"The most common way people give up their power is by thinking they don't have any."
~Alice Walker

Reflection:

Teamwork is defined as the combined action of a group of people—of individuals—that make up a sum.

Teamwork is also considered the collaboration among people working towards a task or a common goal. How the members should work together depends culturally on the perception of the function of a team.

A *compromise* is performed with the understanding that something may have to be given up. *Collaboration* supports the concept that all parties' needs are met.

The perception of the structure and responsibility of each team member's roles also varies with the experience. It's the concept that each member is individually or collectively responsible for each other. How do you perceive it to be?

Activity/Assignment:

How do you define teamwork? Should each member have an equal voice?

Do you ever make a compromise in order to be accepted? If so, what are they? Do you have a strong need to be accepted? Is there a particular group or person that is most important for you to have their acceptance?

Can there be a true collaboration by definition? Have you experienced true collaboration before? How was it accomplished?

Behaviors and Beliefs

"To be yourself in a world that is constantly trying to make you something else is the greatest accomplishment."
~Ralph Waldo Emerson

Reflection:

Behaviors are defined as the way one conducts oneself, especially toward others. What defines good or bad behavior varies among people, groups, and society.

Correct behavior may not always be effective for a particular situation. What is considered valid conduct may not be the most effective. The concept of proper behavior is only successful if the other person feels that is the most effective way, after time spent reflecting on our beliefs and how we express our behaviors because of it.

Activity/Assignment:

What behaviors do you sometimes exhibit when your needs aren't met?

Fill in the reason when you display a particular behavior. Reflect on what is causing you to behave this way. What is typically happening when you act in this manner?

Behavior	When and what causes this?
Over-compensate	
Passive-Aggressive	
Become Angry	
Silent	
Give up easily	
Become controlling or territorial	

Leisure and Pastimes

"Sometimes you need to reconceive yourself, revive hobbies delve into your passion to pursue or catch the best in the world."
~Muzamil Amin

Reflection:

You have hobbies you enjoy that help relieve stress and keep you engaged with life. Having a diversion that's fun helps take your mind off the stresses of daily life.

Leisure time overall enriches our lives. The benefits and importance of pastimes provide a person with the balance needed to focus on all critical aspects of our lives. It improves mental health and wellbeing. Research shows that people with hobbies are less likely to suffer from stress, low mood, and depression.

Leisure times spent listening to or playing music can help manage emotions, help you cope, and create a space to connect with others. Assessing your spare time or even allowing yourself spare time does influence how you perceive your surroundings.

Activity/Assignment:

What are your favorite leisure activities? How do you express yourself?

Fill in the chart to express how you like to spend your spare time—stating your favorite pastimes. You can write in additional pastimes in the spaces provided.

Leisure Activity/ Pastime	What does it allow you to do? How does it make you feel? How does it help?
Music What music do you like? Why? Do you listen, play, or both?	
Arts? What kind?	
Hobbies? What are they?	
Sports? What are they?	

TIME-OUT...PAUSE

You have one last pause and time-out for this section. This section focused on how your beliefs impact how you specifically show up and behave, as well as influence your interaction with others. It has a lot to do with what we might identify as all parts of your personality.

Activity/Assignment:

Rank from best to most challenging how well you are managing the topics. For example, if you feel you do a very good job and that is the best for your well-being, rank that number one and so forth.

Well-Being Topic	Rank
Transformation	
Self-Acceptance	
Responsibility	
Your True North	
Teamwork: Compromising and Collaboration	
Behaviors and Beliefs	
Pastimes	

What will you do to leverage your higher ranked topics against your lower?

What are your AHA moments from this section?

CONGRATULATIONS!
You have successfully completed Stage I: Intentions

Be encouraged and proud of yourself for completing Stage one of three. You have obtained your self-awareness badge. Self-awareness is critical because it helps provide clarity. It will help you understand your thoughts, behaviors, experiences, and even your patterns. In turn, doing this helps you better understand others. Self-awareness is the cornerstone to your development and ability to empathize.

Transition to Stage II:
Take it to the Bridge!

As you prepare to embark on the next section, here are some final preparations and closures.

Please recognize and acknowledge you have done some fantastic work thus far. You have spent a significant amount of time and dedication to doing the PRE (Purpose, Reflection, and Experiences) work with setting your intentions and with how you would like to build better connections with people and become more culturally conscious. There is one last consideration, and that is similarities and differences.

Similarities and differences

There can be so many instances where a person can connect with others and find similarities within processes, artifacts, sayings, and behaviors, then ultimately approach a crossroad with the other in the form of a distinct difference.

A common intersection found is our relationship with food. There are cuisines across cultures that are distinctly different from each other, yet foundationally have some of the same concepts. For example, several cultures have the culinary innovation of dough encasing meat. Jamaica has beef patties, Italy has calzones, Latinx countries like Spain, Colombia, Argentina have empanadas, Russia has pirozhki, South Asia has samosa, Jewish culture has knish, Mongolia has khuushuur, in Lithuania they have Kibinai and all the while in the United States we have Hot Pockets. I could continue to give examples, regardless of name, seasoning, or kind of meat, the cuisine is essentially meat with accompaniments encased in dough. Yet, I would not dare say they are the same to any of these cultures.

It can be extremely easy to emphasize differences between people, groups, or cultures, while equally easy to identify the similarities.

In the next stage, you will be journeying across bridges. Each plank (AKA perspective) will have a crossroad in which we discuss various topics. As you prepare to mount the bridges, I encourage you to not divert to the extreme differences or readily settle on similarities. Find common ground that could be collaborated and respected by all parties while not feeling you are compromising yourself.

Conclusion

There are so many aspects that comprise a person. The goal of this book is to prep you for the next phase of the journey. It defines your "PRE"-work of purpose, reflection, and experiences that empower you to be you.

As you've gone through the first parts of this process, hopefully, you've recognized that no groups of people are monolithic. That many layers and complexities make up each human being.

Activity/Assignment:

Can you be one thing and still another? Are human beings monolithic? Can a group or even a single individual have varying beliefs on different topics?

Monolithic: a group of people who are thought of as being all the same and derived from the word monolith, the Greek word of Monos, meaning "single."

Congratulations again for completing the first stage of the journey!

Stage II: The Bridge

We think in generalities,
but we live in detail.
~Alfred North Whitehead

Stage II: The Bridge

This phase is the work. It's the learning, the engagement, the process, the development, the testing, and research. It's the connecting and linking and the relationship-building.

This portion of the book will identify ways in which you may encounter differences with others. It is these differences that can cause conflict, disagreements and overall disconnect. Each difference is called a "perspective plank." To walk on a bridge, you must walk on the planks to get across. You can walk on each plank or can skip over planks to get across. It is the same with conversations, if you choose to speak up and have a discussion. This is the analogy of walking the bridge. As you engage in conversations of debate or disagreement, you will encounter different reasons for the disagreement or perspective plank. You can discuss each perspective or skip over some.

For example, as I divulged in my bio, I was a very shy child. I didn't smile or talk much, and until I was a young adult, the key color in my wardrobe was black. I remember in my first internship in college, the receptionist told me that I needed to smile more and wear more colors than just black. The receptionist did affirm me by saying I was beautiful, *but* needed to express myself more positively as a young lady by smiling and wearing brighter colors. This was clearly a "bridge moment." Several perspectives, aka planks, were causing her to have this perception.

Each journal entry will specifically address a perspective. Each plank will focus on the concept of that perspective, and how it can have different influences. You will then journal your perspective, with what you learned or from past experiences. You will also explore the views of others, and address any new considerations that you did not recognize prior to the perspective being addressed. The purpose of this stage is to have deeper revelations and potential discussions on how these differences exist, and how conflicts can arise. It is essentially connecting preceding beliefs and values to a perspective.

Perspective planks are the foundation for empathetically thinking about others' mindsets, and how there can be a difference in opinion due to their varying experiences.

During this stage, if the "perspective plank" brings an interest or "aha" moment to your prior knowledge, I encourage you to spend a little more time learning and processing how this improves your paradigm perspective.

The Generalities & Details

The notion that differences fall within a minimal list of issues often only leads to theories that generally become about race and gender. At times, generational distinctions are introduced as the third theoretical description of differences or "diversity." The differences and the conflicts that arise among people are much more significant than this perceived narrow list.

Granted, there is justified logic, reasoning, and evidence about those subjects, and they can be the cornerstones of the conflict. Yet, to identify one of those categories as the sole cause is negligence.

When you encounter a conflict or misunderstanding with a person, you have not approached a bridge. You have hit an impasse. That is where you make decisions on the journey of understanding, collaboration, and empathy.

What should be done now? What will you do? Will you courageously move forward to address the concerns and differences? Will you take the stance of staying in your intentions and ignoring the conflict?

Life is built on the accumulation of the little things. We live by the day-to-day – and it's those events that formulate our thoughts and perceptions. The little things become our details.

The Bridge Concept

What is the bridge theoretically? The bridge is The Opportunity. The bridge is the past journey intentions. It is the traversing and communicating past conflict.

You have successfully accomplished your PRE-Intentions bridge state. Now, you are ready to conquer building and traversing the new.

In this stage, we are going to look at categories in which differences erupt. Differences from western to eastern cultures, inter-regional differences, and interpersonal beliefs and value differences. These topics seem harmless at their face yet can yield concerning, disruptive, and even controversial debate.

Each topic is intended to help realize and acknowledge our complexities and differences, and explore how one portion of a belief can create questions.

The Structure

PERSONALITY			
Traditions	**Institutions**	**Life Experiences**	**Cultural**
Gender	Leadership	Marriage	Societal Values – Norms
Physical/	Workplace Conduct	Divorce	
Mental Abilities		Sickness-Ill-ness-Disease	Creativity: The Arts
Color	Teamwork		Naming
Hair	Personal Space	Death – Dying	Transportation
Children	Feedback –	Grief	Healthcare
Aging	Criticism	Crying	Political – Government
Religion-	Recognition	Drinking – Alcohol	
Spirituality	Concept of Time	Humor	Law – Enforcement
Family	Education	Strangers	Crime & Incar-ceration
Birth Order Preference			Food
Appearance			Colors

The structure has four components: Traditions, Institutions, Life Experiences, and Culture. The concept is based on Marilyn Loden and Judy Rosener's dimensions work and my studies (formally and informally). Loden and Rosener's original study was about diversity dimensions and layers. There have been several adaptations since.

The structure is based on core components that impact our perspective that human beings have levels or dimensions that make them the person they are.

The core of a person is their personality or identity. Who a person is and their genetic makeup overshadows and covers the four components listed above. Each component is an addition to the personality's perspective and the explanation of their viewpoint. It explains the reason or root of the numerous reasons for the make-up and behavior of a person.

You will journey through each component with examples in each. There are plenty more examples within each component and there can be some cross-over between them.

The four core components were developed to make it easy to identify and source the core causes of perception.

Traditions: this component examines your beliefs and ideas that are passed down from one generation to another and give deeper understanding of how you were raised. For example, if you visit homes other than your own, you may find some similarities of practice but still see some definite differences in expected behaviors.

Institutions: this component recognizes that institutions or organizations can impact our perceptions, from education, to employment, to public service, to formalized religious organizations; these are established institutions. For example, in one neighborhood there could be one child bused to an outside public school, another child attending the neighborhood public school, and a third child attending private school. These varied experiences will impact the perception of each child regarding institutionalized establishments.

Life Experiences: this component is the one that affects the broad concept of a person's personality and correlates the most. This is where time plays a vital role in the experiences a person may have. It is the cause and effect also of one's behavior and the consequences of it. An example would be children living in the same home but separated by large gaps of age. In that scenario, they are raised by parents who are at different stages of their own lives, and experiencing events in the world at different ages. Their perception could be different from the siblings who are vastly older or younger than they are.

Cultural: This component examines an overall community or group. It can range from national perspectives to a group as small as a neighborhood. It can include collective social groups that share characteristics, such as nationality or religion. An example would be living in a particular region of the country that identifies with one cultural similarity, but you can still have socio-economic subsets and groups within that same region.

Mile Markers

As you navigate "the bridge," we will identify them as mile markers to commemorate each component accomplished. You will receive a badge to honor your dedication to the journey at the end of each component.

By the end of Stage II, you will have earned four badges of achievement.

- Traditions Badge
- Institutions Badge
- Life Experiences Badge
- Cultural Badge

"The greater our knowledge increases the more our ignorance unfolds."
~John F. Kennedy

Let's aspire to develop and celebrate a broader viewpoint every day.

SEED Communication Method

Don't judge each day by the harvest you reap, but by the seeds you plant.
~Robert Louis Stevenson

I have created the SEED Method, a four-step process to help navigate generalities across perspectives, ideals, behaviors, and beliefs.

This is a resource tool to help you when you encounter a "bridge moment." When you are unsure how to approach the difference, these four steps will help navigate your feelings, encourage empathy, identify opportunities, and assist potential discussions and conversations.

Like any seed, you may not see the immediate return of the outcome to the issue. But by courageously following the seed method, there will be *growth if sown appropriately.*

When you experience different crossroads regarding a topic, use this process. It will help you understand and manage your thoughts and feelings and consider the differing positions of others. Let's look at how to use the tool.

State   Evaluate   Empathize   Decide

STATE	*Stop and state the sense of the situation.*
	What is the situation?
	How did it show up?
	What is the core context?
EVALUATE	*Your opinion?*
	Where is this coming from?
	Are there feelings connected? What are they?
	Is there more you need to find out or learn?
EMPATHIZE	*What are the similarities with the other person?*
	What are the differences?
	What are the other person's emotions?
	How is your behavior / response affecting them?
DECIDE	*Do you want to modify or change?*
	What are you willing to consider?
	Is the other person willing to engage?
	How will you resolve this?

S stands for Stop and State the Situation. This means pausing, taking a time-out from the rhythm of the conversation, and respectfully address-ing the crossroad. It is taking that bridge at that moment to honor the difference.

E stands for Evaluate. This is genuinely addressing the roadblock, the road impasse of your feelings, your true feelings, and defining their origin. It also may be the place to educate yourself as well.

E stands for Empathy. This incorporates emotional intelligence. It is purposefully attempting to understand the other person's point of view, empathizing with their situation.

D stands for Decide. This means genuinely finding an agreement, a common ground. This is deciding what behaviors will be displayed moving forward. The goal isn't necessarily to compromise, meaning a split where you give something and the other person gives something too. It is dis-covering together a collaborative progress. It is an integrative approach. Be mindful; there may be situations where the other party may be unwilling to engage in an educational or productive progression. You still need to utilize the "decide" step. You must decide how healthy the conversation will be if you were to continue. What is the safety of your mental, physical, or spiritual state? If any of these are compromised, you must decide how the closure and next steps will be not imperil your safety. Don't think of this as a failure. There could be several reasons why it is not best to move forward at this time.

The SEED Method is an excellent method to mindfully respect dif-ferences, exercise inclusion, and aspire to equity.

As you progress through each plank (perspective), focus only on that situation and answer the additional questions. Then I challenge you to take that situation to the bridge, especially if you have identified a situation that you have been personally avoiding.

TIME-OUT...PAUSE

Pre-Assessment

We have always held the hope, the belief, the conviction that there is a better life, a better world, beyond the horizon.
~Franklin D. Roosevelt

Activity/Assignment:

Before you begin this stage, pause a moment to review your intent, promise, and pledge."

Summarize below what you think of your journey thus far.

So far, what do you find the most interesting? Most challenging?

TRADITIONS COMPONENT

The traditions dimension follows the core identity (personality) dimension. After you get past the core of who you are, this dimension is about the principal origins impacting your life the most. They are the beliefs that are both handed down and personally taught. The characteristics that result are impossible to avoid because these are the things about yourself you cannot easily change.

Depending on the adaptation, religion is sometimes placed here because there is a substantial dispute that religion is not a negotiable choice for some. Other adaptations have called this layer the internal or personal dimension.

This dimension usually becomes your first line of defense and impact in your life. You are always internally and personally being evaluated, with this component significantly shaping your viewpoints the most.

***Completion of this dimension will award
you the Traditions Badge.***

Discussion:

Gender refers to the social standards, roles, behaviors, characteristics, expressions, and identities traditionally assigned to males and females. Gender is more complex than the medical factors and biological components. Gender becomes more complicated because of the expectations that are associated with it.

Gender roles vary across cultural contexts and daily functions of life. The perspective of the roles can play into a company's policies, practices, and procedures. Roles have changed or progressed in time yet are still managed by the ideal of traditional context.

For example, in Sweden, all working parents are entitled to sixteen months of leave per child, and the "minority" parent takes a minimum of two months of the sixteen. In Japan, approximately 44% of women represent the workforce, yet many women still tend to be pressured to follow traditions and marry.

Gender category systems remain significant cross-culturally. Gender roles with specific tasks traditionally for a woman are typically only accepted for a male if they involve a monetary factor. For example, males learning to sew is not well received traditionally, but if it leads to a profession as a designer, it is better received. Authority is also a gender dynamic that appears in the home, at work, with property rights, and primary governmental, societal, and political power and influence, and these dynamics tend to be based on cultural traditions.

Activity/Assignment:

Practice the SEED Method below. If you have a current situation that you have not been willing to approach regarding this plank, practice "walking this out" here.

SEED Method	Your Perspective
STATE How is this showing up in your life? Family? Friends? Work? Marriage? Children? What is the context for you?	
EVALUATE Your opinion? Where is this coming from? Are there feelings connected? What are they? Is there more you need to learn?	
EMPATHIZE What are your similarities about this with other people? What are the differences? How can the other person feel? How is your behavior/response affecting them?	
DECIDE Do you want to modify or change? What are you willing to consider? How will you resolve any conflicts?	

PERSPECTIVE PLANK
Physical and Mental Abilities

Discussion:

This topic and perspective have evolved and progressed over time. How do we address and assist people with varying abilities?

Terms like "handicapped," "physically challenged," and "differently-abled" were accepted once and still used mainstream today, yet are not the most effective. Learning how to communicate with unfamiliar circumstances can be challenging to address and to provide the understanding and support needed. Focusing on the positive and humanity first is the key.

There are varying statistics that address identifying people with disabilities. The influence spans from covering health, social, and cultural factors. We have witnessed a cultural and world-wide progression in addressing the stigma, protection, and rights of people with physical and mental health differences. The exclusion of this population was frequently identified as shame, a devaluing of their very identity. One of the most significant evolutions is the acknowledgment of their right to make decisions and to fulfill their lives with their distinct abilities.

Activity/Assignment:

Practice the SEED Method below. If you have a current situation that you have not been willing to approach regarding this plank, practice "walking this out" here.

Find people that can be a trusted resource to help you understand behavior that is not familiar to you.

SEED Method	Your Perspective
STATE How is this showing up in your life? Family? Friends? Work? Marriage? Children? What is the context for you?	
EVALUATE Your opinion? Where is this coming from? Are there feelings connected? What are they? Is there more you need to learn?	
EMPATHIZE What are your similarities about this with other people? What are the differences? How can the other person feel? How is your behavior/response affecting them?	
DECIDE Do you want to modify or change? What are you willing to consider? How will you resolve any conflicts?	

Discussion:

The construct of color is an amazing thing! Can you imagine a world without color? From sunsets to sunrises, to a beautiful array of garden flowers, to the mesmerizing colors in an aquarium and the miraculous pigments of birds in a rainforest. They are all exceptional in part because of the ability to display their contrasting hues. I remember my dad discussing how exciting it was when he got his first color television. And think of the effort, time, resources, finances, and research to help those who are physically unable to see color by producing glasses to do just that – help us see in color. Yet, there is sometimes a rigid response to the idea of color with regard to human beings. It is such a predicament that there are established laws and regulations for the protection of such.

As much as we say that color doesn't have a place in society, it does. The color of people is not a singularly siloed issue for one group of people, nation, or culture. It is significantly rooted, and manifests itself frequently, yet is often denied as a reality. Whether there are differences and experiences and patterns of behaviors connected to people of color is a reality—discussed or not.

In Eastern countries, dark skin is considered lower or of a poorer class because of the perceptions of the value of manual labor. Therefore, wearing long sleeves, ski masks, and gloves is common behavior even on the beach. Brazil has the second largest population in which we witness large variances of color, but they fall short in facing the unspoken hierarchal implications of color.

In certain cultures, skin whitening and lightening is very prevalent because of the perception of color. Bleaching skin can bring significant health risks, but individuals practice it because of the social implications of what color represents.

Color has long-standing implications in American history as well from internal and external group dynamics.

The crux of the matter exists in our society. This is a bridge on which a large segment of society does not want to step. Color is a beautiful thing; it is the human attribution of what it can represent that is the issue. Stating that color is seen in a human being is not the resolution.

The perspective varies depending on the hue of the person. Tanning or the luxury of getting darker can be a novelty for some, while it can mean a classification for others.

Activity/Assignment:

Practice the SEED Method below. If you have a current situation that you have not been willing to approach regarding this plank, practice "walking this out" here.

Clearly write out your feelings and viewpoint in the STATE step.

Things to consider:

- Can you see the perspective of skin color being a gap, dimension, and impact for some more than others?
- Has shade or color of skin ever been a topic of conversation? In what context? How was it used?
- Have you approached someone with the topic of skin color you didn't know? What was the context?

SEED Method	Your Perspective
STATE How is this showing up in your life? Family? Friends? Work? Marriage? Children? What is the context for you?	
EVALUATE Your opinion? Where is this coming from? Are there feelings connected? What are they? Is there more you need to learn?	
EMPATHIZE What are your similarities about this with other people? What are the differences? How can the other person feel? How is your behavior/response affecting them?	
DECIDE Do you want to modify or change? What are you willing to consider? How will you resolve any conflicts?	

Hair

Discussion:

Something as indiscriminate as hair would seemingly not be a topic of conflict or impact on society, yet it very much is. The discussion and conversation of hair is associated a lot with the ideals of grooming.

Hair is a part of a person. Yet hair is something that is an insignificant part of our body but can be seen as a political position, epitome of professionalism, or culturally symbolizing spirituality.

Indigenous people have many teachings of the importance and identity of their hair. It is considered sacred and the essence of self-esteem, self-respect, an established sense of belonging, and pride. There are even biblical stories around the identity of hair.

There have been bans, policies, and laws regarding the length or texture of hair. There are structures in place that pretend to define whether how a person's hair grows and is style is considered civilized or respectable. This can also include hair coverings. Women who wear hijabs have often been limited in their ability to engage in sports, and even the concept of style is judged.

Personal self-esteem and sense of vitality can be associate with hair. You may have witnessed a time when friends or family of someone dealing with cancer have displayed solidarity by shaving their own hair. There are some cultures in which the cutting of hair is a spiritual ritual.

Activity/Assignment:

Practice the SEED Method below. If you have a current situation that you have not been willing to approach regarding this plank, practice "walking this out" here.

Things to consider:

- Do you think hair can show respect or disrespect?
- Can hair be sacred?
- Should there be regulations or laws on hair? Should there be protection policies on hair?

SEED Method	Your Perspective
STATE How is this showing up in your life? Family? Friends? Work? Marriage? Children? What is the context for you?	
EVALUATE Your opinion? Where is this coming from? Are there feelings connected? What are they? Is there more you need to learn?	
EMPATHIZE What are your similarities about this with other people? What are the differences? How can the other person feel? How is your behavior/response affecting them?	
DECIDE Do you want to modify or change? What are you willing to consider? How will you resolve any conflicts?	

Children

Discussion:

A child is anyone below the legal age of majority. The concept of a child can change depending on the social and familial norms. This perspective then impacts relationships, responsibilities, rearing, education, the perspective of development, duty to society, family obligation, and the rites of passage to adulthood.

What is considered a normal childhood? How children are raised or reared can vary greatly. Differences can include something as trivial as how they interact with neighbors, whether they earn an allowance, to how parents let them play outside.

In some families there remains an element of older, traditional thoughts of "children are to be seen and not heard." Children raised in this environment will have their behaviors and interactions with others, especially adults, forever shaped. Since child-raising can be a sensitive topic, this plank can be left unventured for SEED growth.

There is a theory called WEIRD (Western, Educated, Industrialized, Rich and Democratic) society and the perspective of how Western society is perceived by Eastern views of child-rearing. Some cultures believe that a child is considered sufficiently advanced by the age of three, and they are left to their own devices.

How can this show up? For example, some in western cultures believe homeschooling or private school is the best a parent can provide for their child if financially able. While some in eastern cultures may feel that having their children live abroad best prepares their child for an economically abundant life.

Activity/Assignment:

Practice the SEED Method below. If you have a current situation that you have not been willing to approach regarding this plank, practice "walking this out" here.

Things to consider:

- How do you see children? Are they just little people, or is there a difference in how they should be managed?
- At what age do you believe a child should be self-sufficient or considered an adult?

SEED Method	Your Perspective
STATE How is this showing up in your life? Family? Friends? Work? Marriage? Children? What is the context for you?	
EVALUATE Your opinion? Where is this coming from? Are there feelings connected? What are they? Is there more you need to learn?	
EMPATHIZE What are your similarities about this with other people? What are the differences? How can the other person feel? How is your behavior/response affecting them?	
DECIDE Do you want to modify or change? What are you willing to consider? How will you resolve any conflicts?	

Aging

Discussion:

The concept of old age and becoming "senior" varies throughout different cultures which have various concepts of the quality of life as one ages. Therefore, the perception of "old age" can range from as young as 50 to as old as 75. The United States has age protection laws that start at age 40.

The use of different words evolves over time. Senior adults are starting to express disapproval of the word "elderly" because it implies feebleness and fragility. As the longevity of life improves, senior care and living arrangements can also bring different perspectives. The concept of how senior adults should be cared for continues to expand.

These changes reflect the culture in which one grew up and also the improvements in our health care that provides for longer, more vibrant senior years. Exchanging views on what our responsibility is to those who need senior care will inevitably bring out different opinions.

The notion of retirement is not a universal concept. Retirement is found to be more practiced in Western and industrialized nations. In Western cultures, retirement is almost always connected to aging, but this is not the case worldwide. Sometimes retirement is associated with the expiration of roles—for example, when one's youngest child is financially on their own. In yet other cultures, retirement comes only in the case of illness and when someone is deemed no longer able contribute to an economy.

Activity/Assignment:

Practice the SEED Method below. If you have a current situation that you have not been willing to approach regarding this plank, practice "walking this out" here.

Things to consider:

- Is there a privilege to being older?
- What are the traditions or behaviors expected with older age for you? Clothes, behavior, etc.
- Do you plan to retire? Do you think people should retire? Should retirement be enforced?

SEED Method	Your Perspective
STATE How is this showing up in your life? Family? Friends? Work? Marriage? Children? What is the context for you?	
EVALUATE Your opinion? Where is this coming from? Are there feelings connected? What are they? Is there more you need to learn?	
EMPATHIZE What are your similarities about this with other people? What are the differences? How can the other person feel? How is your behavior/response affecting them?	
DECIDE Do you want to modify or change? What are you willing to consider? How will you resolve any conflicts?	

Discussion:

The world recognizes 4,300 religions; 83 percent of which are global. There are twelve "classical" or "major religions" across the world and the top two, classified as such by the numbers of people who self-identify with them, are Christianity and Islam.

Religion is a particular system of faith and worship. It is a social-cultural system with an expected set of behaviors, practices, ethics, morals, and views with the relevant guiding text.

Religions themselves can have subgroups which observe their own unique rituals and tenets. For example, someone may identify as a Christian, yet because of their denomination not observe the same rites and doctrines as another Christian denomination. Sometimes the differences are regional.

People who self-identify as "Unaffiliated" comprise the third highest group in this context. This category may include atheists, agnostics, or people who do not identify with any religion but may practice some kinds of religious beliefs and customs.

Activity/Assignment:

Practice the SEED Method below. If you have a current situation that you have not been willing to approach regarding this plank, practice "walking this out" here.

Things to consider:

- Would you consider yourself to believe in a religion?
- What are the critical components of your beliefs?
- Why do you believe what you believe?
- If you have not encountered a situation, research a subgroup of your religion or a completely different belief system than yours. Complete the emphasize section of your SEED step questions.

SEED Method	Your Perspective
STATE How is this showing up in your life? Family? Friends? Work? Marriage? Children? What is the context for you?	
EVALUATE Your opinion? Where is this coming from? Are there feelings connected? What are they? Is there more you need to learn?	
EMPATHIZE What are your similarities about this with other people? What are the differences? How can the other person feel? How is your behavior/response affecting them?	
DECIDE Do you want to modify or change? What are you willing to consider? How will you resolve any conflicts?	

PERSPECTIVE PLANK
Family

Discussion:

The definition of family can be defined much more broadly than a standard dictionary provides. The concept of family is often more than the biological connections that tie human beings together. Overall, "family" can include a group of people who choose to be together and unite with a strong commitment to their bond.

From the blended families that are now celebrated and embraced by society to the historical significance for groups like African American communities that have embraced the holistic purpose of family—those feelings are as profound as biology. The tradition that bestows non-kin titles of "aunt" or "uncle" is part of African American culture, originating from the historical separation of families in slave eras. Latinx cultures, where godparents are highly regarded and involved in their godchildren's lives, are just as important as biological family and are a close circle of distinction.

The unit of a family, however the definition, is where values are originated and set. They are the essence of the tradition of defining right from wrong. The core communication of a family impacts its members' cultural identity and patterns. The better the patterns are understood, the better to navigate the expected behavior.

Activity/Assignment:

Practice the SEED Method below. If you have a current situation that you have not been willing to approach regarding this plank, practice "walking this out" here.

Things to consider:

- What is considered family for you?
- What is your family norm regarding communication? Do you follow that pattern for your immediate family versus a larger circle? Why or why not?
- What are the impacts of your family norm versus others? How would you define your unwritten norms for your circle?
- Do you socialize primarily outside of your family? Why or why not? How does this affect your perspective?

SEED Method	Your Perspective
STATE How is this showing up in your life? Family? Friends? Work? Marriage? Children? What is the context for you?	
EVALUATE Your opinion? Where is this coming from? Are there feelings connected? What are they? Is there more you need to learn?	
EMPATHIZE What are your similarities about this with other people? What are the differences? How can the other person feel? How is your behavior/response affecting them?	
DECIDE Do you want to modify or change? What are you willing to consider? How will you resolve any conflicts?	

Birth Order Preference

Discussion:

An individual's birth order can play a part in forming their perspectives, assumptions, and expectations of themselves and others. Because these expectations are often subconscious, potential conflicts can arise when interacting with others whose experiences may have been different.

Birth order can lead to personality assumptions, theorized traits, and presumed abilities. Family legacy and responsibilities are often assigned differently to the first born as they are to the youngest child. Often the gender of each child is also given a comparable significance when roles are assigned or implied.

Many cultures favor the tradition of a male successor inheriting the family business, along with the designation as "head of the family." Female offspring can be viewed as a burden, especially for lower socio-economic communities, and those beliefs can result in devastating outcomes.

In China, the former one-child policy stemmed from an early attempt to slow a persistent population boom. When combined with a multi-generational belief in a lower value for female offspring, the result was a dark practice of female infanticide.

Gender preference among couples has been included in a Gallup poll question since 1941. In 2013, the American Gallup Poll showed an 8 percent favor for having boys, which is a decrease from the decades before.

Interactions with people who have strong beliefs about a correlation between birth order (or gender) and success in life, can result in conflict.

Activity/Assignment:

Practice the SEED Method below. If you have a current situation that you have not been willing to approach regarding this plank, practice "walking this out" here.

Things to consider:

- Is birth order or gender order and preference important to you?
- How would you have managed a government contributing to your decision to have a child?
- How do you feel about the intention to continue to try to have a child of a specific gender?
- Is this topic important for you?

SEED Method	Your Perspective
STATE How is this showing up in your life? Family? Friends? Work? Marriage? Children? What is the context for you?	
EVALUATE Your opinion? Where is this coming from? Are there feelings connected? What are they? Is there more you need to learn?	
EMPATHIZE What are your similarities about this with other people? What are the differences? How can the other person feel? How is your behavior/response affecting them?	
DECIDE Do you want to modify or change? What are you willing to consider? How will you resolve any conflicts?	

Appearance

Discussion:

Appearance is the way something or someone looks. Appearance is the state, condition, manner, or style of something; it is an outward aspect. Yet, the outer can lead to assumptions about characteristics and status.

The perception of beauty is guided by cultural influences and the concepts of aesthetics. Beauty is described as a feature that is pleasurable to perceive. A personal perception of beauty can impact how people are recognized, treated, mistreated, and even their financial prosperity.

Judgments about appearance can also prejudice a community about a person's competency or ability. For example, a person's body size, either their height or their weight, can affect how they are perceived and judged.

Activity/Assignment:

Practice the SEED Method below. If you have a current situation that you have not been willing to approach regarding this plank, practice "walking this out" here.

Things to consider:

- Have you had discussions about appearance? If so, what are they usually about?
- Has appearance personally impacted your life?
- How much merit do you place on appearance? How do you regard people that have prejudices about appearance?

SEED Method	Your Perspective
STATE How is this showing up in your life? Family? Friends? Work? Marriage? Children? What is the context for you?	
EVALUATE Your opinion? Where is this coming from? Are there feelings connected? What are they? Is there more you need to learn?	
EMPATHIZE What are your similarities about this with other people? What are the differences? How can the other person feel? How is your behavior/response affecting them?	
DECIDE Do you want to modify or change? What are you willing to consider? How will you resolve any conflicts?	

CONGRATULATIONS
on earning your second Badge!

TRADITIONS BADGE

TIME-OUT...PAUSE

Congratulations on purposefully being present and conscious regarding your aspects and components of your life. You have navigated through the potential impact and experience of the internal and primary dimensions of your life.

This internal aspect may influence your behavior and how you engage in society. You have deliberately spent priceless time consciously addressing your conscious and subconscious feelings regarding quite common life matters that can't be avoided and must be dealt with in your life.

Gender
Physical and Mental Abilities
Color
Hair
Children
Aging
Religion-Spirituality
Family
Birth Order Preference
Appearance

How has this dimension shown up in your life?	
Which "perspective plank" did you resonate with the most? Why?	
How can knowledge and awareness help you?	

INSTITUTIONAL COMPONENT

The institutional dimension is after the traditions dimension. This section is the third impactful experience that will influence your perspective. It can be the work formal organizational perspective. As an adult, most of your life and day is spent in your place of employment. Your experiences and roles do influence your ideals of life. Therefore, referencing educational systems consequently represents all generational representation and experience.

Completion of this dimension will award you the Institutions Badge.

PERSPECTIVE PLANK
Leadership

Discussion:

Leadership is the art of motivating a group of people to act. The art or the style a leader displays can influence how one is accepted by society.

The concept of leadership is universal, yet the expectations and principles of a leader changes with the environment that is enforcing the quality traits. There are core components most look for in leaders, yet there are traits and attributes found in the context of the culture. How a leader communicates, makes decisions, and encourages relationships can be a key to the quality of the climate of the organization.

If a person can inspire a group of people to follow them, they have a high level of social intelligence. They understand the dynamics required to embrace and accept that leader's direction. How the leader does that and how it affects the follower is subject to individual interpretation.

There is a growing trend in understanding intergenerational leadership. The intent is that there needs to be a continuous generational awareness of how a person leads the organizational structure and workplace composition. For the first time in history, an organization can have up to four to five generations in one workplace. Generations are only one aspect of how successful leadership can be perceived.

There are several aspects about what constitutes a good leader. High levels of competency with communication, relationships, and style of managing all are factors.

Activity/Assignment:

Practice the SEED Method below. If you have a current situation that you have not been willing to approach regarding this plank, practice "walking this out" here.

Things to consider:

- Have you experienced an environment that encourages a leadership style you were not agreeable to?
- Do you influence the way you were led when you were younger? What are the similarities and differences?
- What aspects, traits, qualities do you look for in a leader? Have you encountered the opposite?
- What attributes do you believe do not make up a great leader?

SEED Method	Your Perspective
STATE How is this showing up in your life? Family? Friends? Work? Marriage? Children? What is the context for you?	
EVALUATE Your opinion? Where is this coming from? Are there feelings connected? What are they? Is there more you need to learn?	
EMPATHIZE What are your similarities about this with other people? What are the differences? How can the other person feel? How is your behavior/response affecting them?	
DECIDE Do you want to modify or change? What are you willing to consider? How will you resolve any conflicts?	

Workplace Conduct

Discussion:

There are common workplace standards and characteristics that are considered appropriate at work. Behavior at work can differ by the type of work that a person is performing. This conduct is often described as professionalism.

Professionalism is defined as the conduct, aims, or qualities that characterize or make a profession. A professional attitude is considered a more formal approach to relationships. Professionalism is viewed as a skill because it must be learned to adapt to the person's expected environment. It is a combination of behaviors that a group or an authority expects the person to adhere to in that work setting.

Workplace conduct and behavior expectations can change depending on the physical or functional differences of a company. The varying locations of the work being conducted can redefine acceptable workplace behavior or professionalism. Even within that same industry, there can be different definitions of what professionalism should look like.

Culture affects workplace conduct because of the values that may influence them. If there is a high value placed on relationships versus work, or vice versa, employees' behaviors need to modify to fit the accepted standards of their workplace.

Activity/Assignment:

Practice the SEED Method below. If you have a current situation that you have not been willing to approach regarding this plank, practice "walking this out" here.

Things to consider:

- Have you been challenged by a transition of working for an organization and then moved to a different location, and had to modify your processes to adapt to the changed environment? Did you adjust? How?

- What is acceptable workplace conduct? What is unacceptable workplace conduct?

- Do you consider professionalism the same as workplace behavior, or different? Is professionalism only necessary for certain people?

SEED Method	Your Perspective
STATE How is this showing up in your life? Family? Friends? Work? Marriage? Children? What is the context for you?	
EVALUATE Your opinion? Where is this coming from? Are there feelings connected? What are they? Is there more you need to learn?	
EMPATHIZE What are your similarities about this with other people? What are the differences? How can the other person feel? How is your behavior/response affecting them?	
DECIDE Do you want to modify or change? What are you willing to consider? How will you resolve any conflicts?	

PERSPECTIVE PLANK
Teamwork

Discussion:

Teamwork is the concept of everyone working together for a common goal and was discussed in Stage I: Intentions as well.

The perception each person has of teamwork plays a significant role in the working relationships they form with each other. The success of a team depends on a shared perception of the importance of the work, the project, and input from others. When there is not a common level of work ethic, or a shared concept of the importance of the project, it is possible that one member will provide only the minimum effort required to get the work done, while others diligently go above and beyond to excel.

Our perspective can be a part of the core concept of who we intrinsically are. One person may become naturally collaborative, while another person can be more analytical, focusing on the details, and yet another may be more inclined to take an independent stance. These three will have a clash of perspectives.

The SEED method is especially needed for this plank (perspective). Taking the time to consider each other's viewpoint, expectation, and vision for the team is important. Following the process will help decide what type of team the group wants to be. Being proactive is a great best practice.

Activity/Assignment:

Practice the SEED Method below. If you have a current situation that you have not been willing to approach regarding this plank, practice "walking this out" here.

Things to consider:

- Have you faced challenges being on a team? What were they?
- Review your comments on teams in Stage I. What were the highlights?

SEED Method	Your Perspective
STATE How is this showing up in your life? Family? Friends? Work? Marriage? Children? What is the context for you?	
EVALUATE Your opinion? Where is this coming from? Are there feelings connected? What are they? Is there more you need to learn?	
EMPATHIZE What are your similarities about this with other people? What are the differences? How can the other person feel? How is your behavior/response affecting them?	
DECIDE Do you want to modify or change? What are you willing to consider? How will you resolve any conflicts?	

Personal Space

Discussion:

Personal space is essentially the physical distance between people in a social, family, and work environment. Intrusion in personal space, especially in the context of being at work, can cause the work environment to be at the brink of persistent conflict (a bridge).

While accommodating personal space is a social skill, it is practiced under the norms and interactions of social dynamics. Not only are there social dynamics regarding personal space, but there are also new studies in neuroscience and psychology that conclude the brain and body respond as well.

From a psychological standpoint, comfort with interpersonal distance or space is influenced by mindset and relationships. Personal proximity can feel territorial. A person who has become comfortable sitting at a specific seat in a meeting room may feel uncomfortable for the duration of a meeting if someone else chooses that chair. The middle seat in an airplane row can create similar discomfort for a person who feels the need for more personal space.

Personal space discussed in this organizational dimension is important because this perspective may show up frequently during common expectations of work and relationships.

Activity/Assignment:

Practice the SEED Method below. If you have a current situation that you have not been willing to approach regarding this plank, practice "walking this out" here.

Things to consider:

- Do you need personal space?
- Is there someone that you believe invades your space? Why do you feel this way?
- Are you aware of this being a need for others?

SEED Method	Your Perspective
STATE How is this showing up in your life? Family? Friends? Work? Marriage? Children? What is the context for you?	
EVALUATE Your opinion? Where is this coming from? Are there feelings connected? What are they? Is there more you need to learn?	
EMPATHIZE What are your similarities about this with other people? What are the differences? How can the other person feel? How is your behavior/response affecting them?	
DECIDE Do you want to modify or change? What are you willing to consider? How will you resolve any conflicts?	

PERSPECTIVE PLANK
Feedback – Communication – Criticism

Discussion:

Feedback provides information about a person's performance with the intention of helping improve the relationship, situation, or task. Unfortunately, feedback is not always felt or welcomed for what it is intended to be.

Feedback can be tough to accomplish and navigate; therefore, it is often avoided. The avoidance happens because the fear of embarking on a discussion bridge could lead to negative outcomes.

Some people and cultures do not believe their subordinates should advise a person of authority. Therefore, many employees may never truly offer their boss feedback, even if asked. The employee has an inner conflict between following the manager's request for feedback, and their belief that it is disrespectful to give a person of authority recommendations. The decision of what the employee will do is heavily influenced by the experiences they've had in other situations that may have changed or confirmed their perspective. Therefore, the SEED Method is important. It will help you decide whether to modify, keep or change your perspective.

Before you can effectively provide feedback, you have to know how you feel about feedback. Suppose you are not aware of your feelings. Your behavior will reflect the uncertainty of your feelings, both consciously and unconsciously. The receiver of your advice will respond with their own past experiences. Learning more about the person, their perspectives, experiences, and perhaps some cultural norms can help you have a better relationship with them and effectively provide feedback.

Activity/Assignment:

Practice the SEED Method below. If you have a current situation that you have not been willing to approach regarding this plank, practice "walking this out" here.

Things to consider:

- How have people reacted when you have given them feedback? What do you believe are the reasons why they responded the way they did?
- How do you feel about feedback?
- The people you interact with - do you know how they feel and prefer feedback?

SEED Method	Your Perspective
STATE How is this showing up in your life? Family? Friends? Work? Marriage? Children? What is the context for you?	
EVALUATE Your opinion? Where is this coming from? Are there feelings connected? What are they? Is there more you need to learn?	
EMPATHIZE What are your similarities about this with other people? What are the differences? How can the other person feel? How is your behavior/response affecting them?	
DECIDE Do you want to modify or change? What are you willing to consider? How will you resolve any conflicts?	

Recognition

Discussion:

Recognition was a topic you reflected on in Stage I: Intentions. It is repeated here because it is important to understand the lingering impact that negatively received recognition can have within an institutional setting, whether employment or educational.

It is even more important for this dimension because these are situations where people (students or employees) are officially expected to perform. If there isn't a conscious effort to understand how to motivate a person and know how to effectively acknowledge them within an organization, it can be collectively detrimental.

Every institution needs to have a recognition strategy. This should include understanding the perceptions of recognition by its constituents. Recognition programs should have different methods for accommodating the various ways people like to be recognized.

Thinking in a formal setting like work, school, or even volunteer groups, reflect on their recognition program(s). Think about programs that you experienced in the past. Were they successful? Why or why not? Determining if they were successful depends on the perspective of that person.

If recognition is not discussed and all parties have not considered the needs and expectations of others, morale can be diminished.

Activity/Assignment:

Practice the SEED Method below. If you have a current situation that you have not been willing to approach regarding this plank, practice "walking this out" here.

Things to consider:

- What are typical responses that you hear when people are not happy with how they are recognized?
- Has recognition personally impacted you in life? How?
- How important do you believe recognition to be? Do you believe recognition should be earned?

SEED Method	Your Perspective
STATE How is this showing up in your life? Family? Friends? Work? Marriage? Children? What is the context for you?	
EVALUATE Your opinion? Where is this coming from? Are there feelings connected? What are they? Is there more you need to learn?	
EMPATHIZE What are your similarities about this with other people? What are the differences? How can the other person feel? How is your behavior/response affecting them?	
DECIDE Do you want to modify or change? What are you willing to consider? How will you resolve any conflicts?	

PERSPECTIVE PLANK
Concept of Time

Discussion:

The concept of time varies across cultures. Time can be looked at as a limited resource which must be precisely scheduled. A limited resource is often thought of as multi-purposeful; therefore, the quality of time spent with people is a gift. The other end of the spectrum in perceiving time is to consider time as plentiful and that it shouldn't be controlled, but rather allowed to flow naturally. The concept of rushing is not contemplated at all.

How do these differences show up at work? You may have a person who believes that the concept of time is plentiful; therefore, making quick decisions is challenging for them because they believe extra time should be taken to thoroughly examine every option. If you have a person that believes in the concept of time being multi-purposeful, they will honor the time together, but they may have a completely different concept of a schedule or may even be late for a meeting because they were multitasking. The person who feels like time is a limited resource will be frustrated with parties that feel there is always plenty of time.

The concept is subjective. It can be seen differently by Eastern and Western cultures and, of course, within groups and the functions of each group.

The pace and the orientation of time can come from long historical situations. Some countries may have a transit system that can be hours to even a full day late and the people have adapted to that system. The concept of how you use your time can be subject to debate. The use of time is a very subjective topic.

Activity/Assignment:

Practice the SEED Method below. If you have a current situation that you have not been willing to approach regarding this plank, practice "walking this out" here.

Things to consider:

- Are there certain occasions where time is more important to you?
- Have you worked with people that have seen time differently than you? How did you manage it?
- Do you know someone that is challenging to work with or relate to because of their concept of time?

SEED Method	Your Perspective
STATE How is this showing up in your life? Family? Friends? Work? Marriage? Children? What is the context for you?	
EVALUATE Your opinion? Where is this coming from? Are there feelings connected? What are they? Is there more you need to learn?	
EMPATHIZE What are your similarities about this with other people? What are the differences? How can the other person feel? How is your behavior/response affecting them?	
DECIDE Do you want to modify or change? What are you willing to consider? How will you resolve any conflicts?	

Education

Discussion:

Perceptions of education can have cultural foundations or might reflect a family's history, economic level, and their community's involvement. The posture on private versus public institutions vary as well.

Across the world more than 72 million children at the primary level do not attend school. 759 million adults are illiterate. Overall, worldwide, girls have the least access to education. In the United States, women are more likely to enroll in and complete college than men, resulting in an average of 7 percent more women than men having higher education degrees. This crosses ethnic and racial groups. Some countries do not charge for attending college so it is not unusual for residents of the United States, or other countries with high tuition costs, to study abroad to take advantage of those opportunities. College tuition in the United States has doubled since the 1980s, increasing at a faster rate than wage increases.

There are studies that show that homeschooling is on the rise, with the availability of virtual platforms and assistance.

This level of institutional perspective will be more evident with the experience of the pandemic, some children were less impacted than others, some students in smaller or private institutions were able continue in-person education while the larger populated schools were all virtual.

Education perspective will transcend all the way to work with how a person learns, to how they interact socially and how authority is valued.

Activity/Assignment:

Practice the SEED Method below. If you have a current situation that you have not been willing to approach regarding this plank, practice "walking this out" here.

Things to consider:

- What makes a good education?
- How do you think education should be managed?
- Should education be available for all or only to certain levels?

SEED Method	Your Perspective
STATE How is this showing up in your life? Family? Friends? Work? Marriage? Children? What is the context for you?	
EVALUATE Your opinion? Where is this coming from? Are there feelings connected? What are they? Is there more you need to learn?	
EMPATHIZE What are your similarities about this with other people? What are the differences? How can the other person feel? How is your behavior/response affecting them?	
DECIDE Do you want to modify or change? What are you willing to consider? How will you resolve any conflicts?	

CONGRATULATIONS,
You have completed your third competence badge!

TIME-OUT...PAUSE

Congratulations on obtaining your third badge! From the educational institutions where we learn to the organizations where we work; all impact the way we behave and perceive. You are doing a great job of addressing the common detail of discourse.

Leadership
Workplace Conduct
Teamwork
Personal Space
Feedback – Communication - Criticism
Recognition
Concept of Time
Education

How has this dimension shown up in your life?	
Which "perspective plank" did you resonate the most with? Why?	
How can knowledge and awareness now help you?	

LIFE EXPERIENCES COMPONENT

The *life experiences affect your perspective after the institutions dimension. The influence is next because it is the concepts of things you have experienced in life. Where you live, the language you speak, the kind of education attained, the style of common communication, your relationship status with family, marital and parental. Other adaptations have referenced this dimension as community and external dimensions.*

Completion of this dimension will award you the Life Experiences' Badge

Marriage

Discussion:

A person's perception and expectations of marriage are influenced by their personal experiences. The perception may be partially determined by their gender, status in society, religious beliefs, and, quite often, political affiliation.

And studies show that the concept of marriage can change as society evolves and communities are more willing to embrace alliances that were at one timed deemed improper.

The construct of marriage has changed over centuries. In its early establishment, marriage was an agreement and alliance between families, often to solidify economic liaisons. Arranged marriages still exist today, but now they are typically not forced on the couple. Fifty-five percent of marriages across the globe are arranged marriages. Therefore, these marriages are relevant in all countries.

It is more common today for couples to delay marriage. Some choose not to marry at all yet may still be in a long, committed relationship. The traditional construct of marriage and the societal stigma of being unwed have impacted the behavior and perspective of marriage.

Perspective on marriage delicately affects others by their own experience of how successful or challenging and it is displayed in behavior.

Activity/Assignment:

Practice the SEED Method below. If you have a current situation that you have not been willing to approach regarding this plank, practice "walking this out" here.

Things to consider:

- How do you see marriage?
- Has your perspective changed over the years?
- Do you see marriage and responsibilities of marriage differently than the elders in your personal life?
- Do you know of anyone that has a different perspective than you?

SEED Method	Your Perspective
STATE How is this showing up in your life? Family? Friends? Work? Marriage? Children? What is the context for you?	
EVALUATE Your opinion? Where is this coming from? Are there feelings connected? What are they? Is there more you need to learn?	
EMPATHIZE What are your similarities about this with other people? What are the differences? How can the other person feel? How is your behavior/response affecting them?	
DECIDE Do you want to modify or change? What are you willing to consider? How will you resolve any conflicts?	

PERSPECTIVE PLANK
Divorce

Discussion:

There are strong feelings and beliefs when it comes to the topic of divorce. They are impactful because there are significant repercussions, consequences, and value system impacts on this topic.

Overall, divorce is almost universally seen as something negative, and yet it is common among most cultures. One position might be that it would have been better if a person never got married than having a marriage end in divorce. The implications of never marrying might have lower consequences than divorcing. Divorce can result in ostracization by family, or division in mutual friend circles.

Some studies suggest that the more modernized or industrialized an environment, the higher potential for divorce. The economic dependency of marriage is not needed; therefore, people are not staying in the marriage for financial stability.

Baby Boomers are divorcing at a rate double their earlier rate, to the point they are being dubbed as "gray divorces." At the same time, Generation X and especially Millennials are dropping the divorce rate by 18 percent from 2008 to 2016. The large disparity appears to be found in the fact that Boomers typically got married at an early age and now live longer than previous generations. They appear to be questioning their desire to continue such a long pairing. The younger generations with the lower divorce rates are marrying later and thus taking their vows after taking time to mature and settle into their personal beliefs and perspectives on marriage.

This topic may be emotionally triggering for some. Learning how to evaluate your feelings and opinions can help you find the gaps where you may need more healing. It will also help you when these discussions arise, and you can wisely be present for the conversation and not be distracted by triggers that have not been fully processed.

Realizing that a person's experience throughout their life regarding divorce effects how they may enter their own intimate relationships and perspective of defending the idea of divorce.

Activity/Assignment:

Practice the SEED Method below. If you have a current situation that you have not been willing to approach regarding this plank, practice "walking this out" here.

Things to consider:

- What are your feelings regarding divorce?
- Do you have certain beliefs about divorce? Do you think your beliefs are realistic?
- Do you think others feel differently? Why do you think they feel that way?

SEED Method	Your Perspective
STATE How is this showing up in your life? Family? Friends? Work? Marriage? Children? What is the context for you?	
EVALUATE Your opinion? Where is this coming from? Are there feelings connected? What are they? Is there more you need to learn?	
EMPATHIZE What are your similarities about this with other people? What are the differences? How can the other person feel? How is your behavior/response affecting them?	
DECIDE Do you want to modify or change? What are you willing to consider? How will you resolve any conflicts?	

PERSPECTIVE PLANK
Sickness – Illness – Disease

Discussion:

Sickness is the state of being ill. Illness does play a role in how society functions. Disease can adversely affect a person's body, mind and sense of self. How society responds to that condition plays a substantial role in respecting, and even accepting those we encounter.

Sometimes blame plays a part in in interactions with others. Occasionally the patient is blamed, or accused of being responsible for their illness, while other forms of illness are perceived as blameless and unable to be controlled. The placement of blame can undermine the compassion given to a person, and can even lead to delayed treatment. A prime example of this was when the initial epidemic of HIV AIDS was diagnosed.

There are family values within cultures that may promote withholding a diagnosis or prognosis of a sick relative. The belief that family members should shield a sick person from the burden of the information and for them to bear it themselves, is grounded in the theory that hearing the bad news, or talking about the possibility of death, could lead to a worse outcome.

The idea of managing pain and the level of fighting the illness are often perceived differently by culture. Therefore, the perception and expression of pain may manifest differently by the person who is sick.

These instilled perceptions can show up in daily life, including the difference between calling in sick or coming to work sick. Perceptions can affect decisions about the level of treatment and intervention with a disease. And they can cause confusion with regard to communicating with a sick friend, or choosing to discuss that illness with others.

Activity/Assignment:

Practice the SEED Method below. If you have a current situation that you have not been willing to approach regarding this plank, practice "walking this out" here.

Things to consider:

- Is there a time where you think modern medicine should not intervene with an illness or disease?
- Should pain be completely avoided at all costs for the patient?
- Do you like others (outside of your close circle) to know when you are ill or sick?
- Do you allow your loved ones to know when you are in pain?

SEED Method	Your Perspective
STATE How is this showing up in your life? Family? Friends? Work? Marriage? Children? What is the context for you?	
EVALUATE Your opinion? Where is this coming from? Are there feelings connected? What are they? Is there more you need to learn?	
EMPATHIZE What are your similarities about this with other people? What are the differences? How can the other person feel? How is your behavior/response affecting them?	
DECIDE Do you want to modify or change? What are you willing to consider? How will you resolve any conflicts?	

PERSPECTIVE PLANK
Death and Dying

Discussion:

Death and dying are inevitable in everyone's life, yet it can be a complex and challenging discussion for some. Death can often be a taboo for discussion.

Lately, there has been a shift regarding the notion of death. Within America, Baby Boomers, at a higher rate than previous generations, are becoming more open with discussion and preplanning of their funerals so their passing and burial can be on their own terms.

According to the National Funeral Director Association, only twenty-one percent of Americans have spoken to loved ones regarding their death. There is a growing group of millennials that are seeing discussion of death more positively. Apps and organizations have been founded on this positive premise have a healthy conversation regarding death and dying.

Death and dying are being reconsidered when it comes to burial as well. There are growing numbers who are seeking burials that are more environmentally conscious, for example. People are choosing cremation at higher rates, dedicating their bodies to science, and choosing living urns that are trees or cemeteries becoming memory forests. Cremations are up by eight percent, while burials are down seven percent.

This topic may be unnerving for some. At the same time, some cultures discuss and embrace death as a part of life. Some cultures will have celebrations honoring loved ones that have died. The perception of death is changing by generation, and addressing this bridge or conflict when this arises would be advantageous.

Reflecting on yours and other experiences regarding death and dying is one that will be unavoidable, therefore a needed topic to process.

Activity/Assignment:

Practice the SEED Method below. If you have a current situation that you have not been willing to approach regarding this plank, practice "walking this out" here.

Things to consider:

- How do you feel about death?
- Do you discuss death or dying with others?
- How would you feel if someone openly and regularly talked about death, those who have died, and the concept of dying?

SEED Method	Your Perspective
STATE How is this showing up in your life? Family? Friends? Work? Marriage? Children? What is the context for you?	
EVALUATE Your opinion? Where is this coming from? Are there feelings connected? What are they? Is there more you need to learn?	
EMPATHIZE What are your similarities about this with other people? What are the differences? How can the other person feel? How is your behavior/response affecting them?	
DECIDE Do you want to modify or change? What are you willing to consider? How will you resolve any conflicts?	

Grief

Discussion:

Grief is a natural reaction to a loss. It is universal. Grief can be from any loss, the death and loss of a loved one, ending an important relationship, job loss, loss of independence, loss of a prized possession, or loss of a companion. What is considered a normal way to grieve is dependent on cultural norms.

Grief can be complex because it is deeply personal, yet it is entangled with the norms of the culture, the person's status and expectations, or the person's position in the context of an institution.

The merely expected behavior of how to show grief is defined by a cultural society. While some expect a response of reverence and quiet in mourning, others fully display their raw emotions openly.

Even though grief can have influences within certain cultures and traditions, a persons own personal experience and journey will significantly impact their ability and ideals to managing grief.

Activity/Assignment:

Practice the SEED Method below. If you have a current situation that you have not been willing to approach regarding this plank, practice "walking this out" here.

Things to consider:

- How does your society accept grief?
- How are you expected to grieve personally? How has grief personally impacted your life?
- Do you feel like expressing your grief the way that is best for you?

SEED Method	Your Perspective
STATE How is this showing up in your life? Family? Friends? Work? Marriage? Children? What is the context for you?	
EVALUATE Your opinion? Where is this coming from? Are there feelings connected? What are they? Is there more you need to learn?	
EMPATHIZE What are your similarities about this with other people? What are the differences? How can the other person feel? How is your behavior/response affecting them?	
DECIDE Do you want to modify or change? What are you willing to consider? How will you resolve any conflicts?	

Crying

Discussion:

Crying is the shedding of tears or welling of tears in the eyes. Crying is the physical response to an emotional state of a person. There can be a variety of emotions that lead to crying— gratitude, sadness, happiness, anger, pain, or frustration - these are all examples that may result in tears. WebMD says that "shedding tears can be good for your health—especially in the right setting."

This shows a variety of the negative way people talk about crying:

- Crying can have cultural implications.
- Crying is unprofessional and never should happen at work.
- Crying is a weakness; men especially shouldn't do it.
- Crying is used as a weapon, and certain gender and races use it to manipulate.

The idea and concept of crying is heavily influenced by how society supports it. There are studies that state it is healthy to cry. It also says that crying "activates" the body in a good way. For example, Japan has "crying clubs." People get together for the sole purpose of crying. The benefits are better mental health and a better nervous system; it restores the body's state of balance, regulates your mood, detoxes the body, and helps you recover from grief.

Studies say it is unhealthy to resist the urge to cry. WebMD says, "(we are) doing ourselves a disservice by not tearing up regularly."

Author's note: Am I the only one that noticed the word "regularly?" Who cries regularly? Am I missing out on something? Should I be crying regularly? How often is regular? Like anything, you can have too much. It's about moderation.

Maybe the songwriter was all wrong in saying, "Don't cry out loud, just keep it inside."

Crying is truly subjective to how a person experiences responses to them crying and it can be situational in experience. Truly reflecting how you have responded to others crying and how others have responded to you will impact your perspective.

Activity/Assignment:

Practice the SEED Method below. If you have a current situation that you have not been willing to approach regarding this plank, practice "walking this out" here.

Things to consider:

- What is the truth regarding crying for you? How do you feel about it?
- What are your overall thoughts and beliefs about crying?
- Are there appropriate and inappropriate times to cry? Is there an appropriate or inappropriate way to cry?
- Do you believe there is an age limit to crying?

SEED Method	Your Perspective
STATE How is this showing up in your life? Family? Friends? Work? Marriage? Children? What is the context for you?	
EVALUATE Your opinion? Where is this coming from? Are there feelings connected? What are they? Is there more you need to learn?	
EMPATHIZE What are your similarities about this with other people? What are the differences? How can the other person feel? How is your behavior/response affecting them?	
DECIDE Do you want to modify or change? What are you willing to consider? How will you resolve any conflicts?	

PERSPECTIVE PLANK
Drinking – Alcohol

Discussion:

Alcohol use can be perceived in different ways depending on culture and beliefs. Belgium, Italy, Switzerland, and Spain allow some form of alcohol consumption as early as age 16. While some countries and religions entirely ban the consumption of alcohol.

Some studies claim that the behavioral effects of alcohol are actually a result of the social and cultural factors rather than your body's chemical reaction to the alcohol. But where alcohol is allowed, drinking is nearly universally associated with celebrations.

Ten countries ban alcohol consumption, and at one time, the United States did the same during the Prohibition era. There are still states in the U. S. that have "blue laws," which govern the alcohol content and the days in which alcohol can be purchased.

Alcohol can be a sensitive topic for people who may have experienced negative consequences in their life due to alcohol consumption or exposure. Alcohol is a plank (perspective) that can socially place you at the bridge of conflict to cross.

The experiences that a person has regarding alcohol heavily impacts their socialization, relationships and overall engagement with others.

Activity/Assignment:

Practice the SEED Method below. If you have a current situation that you have not been willing to approach regarding this plank, practice "walking this out" here.

Things to consider:

- Have you ever consumed alcohol?
- What are your reasons for drinking or not alcohol?
- Do you like to socialize with alcohol? What are your reasons?
- Do you agree with the governance of the consumption of alcohol?

SEED Method	Your Perspective
STATE How is this showing up in your life? Family? Friends? Work? Marriage? Children? What is the context for you?	
EVALUATE Your opinion? Where is this coming from? Are there feelings connected? What are they? Is there more you need to learn?	
EMPATHIZE What are your similarities about this with other people? What are the differences? How can the other person feel? How is your behavior/response affecting them?	
DECIDE Do you want to modify or change? What are you willing to consider? How will you resolve any conflicts?	

PERSPECTIVE PLANK
Humor

Discussion:

Humor is a state of mind or mood where a person finds something amusing, funny, or entertaining.

Culture impacts a person's perception of humor and how it is used, generating varying degrees of acceptance and non-acceptance. Western culture has a more positive embrace of humor than Eastern counterparts. Humor is considered a universal human attribute, yet how it should be used is subject to cultural interpretation.

Humor can be viewed as an indication of a well-adjusted person, while in some cultures, it's seen as less honorable. And a joke about life's mishaps might be received by one person as a way to lighten a dark mood, while another may take offense and have an angry reaction.

How a person has experienced various forms of humor will impact their expectation of how humor should be expressed among others.

Activity/Assignment:

Practice the SEED Method below. If you have a current situation that you have not been willing to approach regarding this plank, practice "walking this out" here.

Things to consider:

- What do you find funny?
- Do you easily get offended by jokes?
- What do you think are things that should not be taken as funny or humorous? Are some things off-limits?
- Are you the one who often tries to be humorous?

SEED Method	Your Perspective
STATE How is this showing up in your life? Family? Friends? Work? Marriage? Children? What is the context for you?	
EVALUATE Your opinion? Where is this coming from? Are there feelings connected? What are they? Is there more you need to learn?	
EMPATHIZE What are your similarities about this with other people? What are the differences? How can the other person feel? How is your behavior/response affecting them?	
DECIDE Do you want to modify or change? What are you willing to consider? How will you resolve any conflicts?	

PERSPECTIVE PLANK
Strangers

Discussion:

A stranger is generally described as a person who isn't known or familiar with regard to a group of people or a specific place. The word stranger derives from the Middle French word *estrangier*, meaning a foreigner or alien. The boundaries about who is considered a stranger vary culturally.

How do you behave and react to someone you don't know? Do you greet them, ignore them, confront them, isolate from them? Do you reach out to help them if it appears they are in need? In the context of hospitality, when does a perception of a person change from stranger to guest?

Some cultures are more open about embracing a stranger and viewing the encounter as a chance to learn. The concept of a stranger can be influenced by the religious teachings one values as well.

In the United States in the 1980s, the term "stranger danger" was popularized. This was created to help fight against the epidemic of child kidnappings and murders. This was a relatively new social transition—this fear of trusting people who may encounter our children. Now there is a new evolution that shifts back to generalized trust in strangers. We are essentially trusting strangers when we ride an Uber® or Lyft®. We trust strangers when we invite them to our front door with Door Dash®, Grubhub®, or UberEats®.

Activity/Assignment:

The cultural concept of a stranger also affects the willingness to help someone if we notice a need. Research has shown that helping strangers in different cultures was inversely related to a country's economic productivity. There are many aspects to how someone would perceive a stranger; the largest component would be how they have encountered others in their past. Things to consider:

- How do you naturally respond to individuals or groups who are different from you? What do you believe causes this?
- What factors influence your choice to engage with a person you don't know?
- What can you learn from people who have grown up with religions, cultures, and habits that are different from your own?

SEED Method	Your Perspective
STATE How is this showing up in your life? Family? Friends? Work? Marriage? Children? What is the context for you?	
EVALUATE Your opinion? Where is this coming from? Are there feelings connected? What are they? Is there more you need to learn?	
EMPATHIZE What are your similarities about this with other people? What are the differences? How can the other person feel? How is your behavior/response affecting them?	
DECIDE Do you want to modify or change? What are you willing to consider? How will you resolve any conflicts?	

CONGRATULATIONS,
You have completed your fourth competency badge!

TIME-OUT...PAUSE

You have earned your next Badge! Congratulations! You only have one badge left. This section may have been more challenging for you – it was certainly larger. You reviewed the day-to-day functions in your life that you may not have noticed that are situational in perspective. You should be proud of yourself for your dedication.

Marriage
Divorce
Sickness
Death and Dying
Grief
Crying
Drinking
Humor
Strangers

How has this dimension shown up in your life?	
Which "perspective plank" did you resonate the most with? Why?	
How can knowledge and awareness now help you?	

CULTURAL COMPONENT

As we collectively become smaller globally in communications, transit, and work, this will have a larger cross-cultural impact. This dimension addresses the norms and nuisances of the broader structural context and culture. Other adaptations have considered this to be social life experience, global and collective dimension.

Completion of this dimension will award you the Cultural Badge.

PERSPECTIVE PLANK
Societal Values – Cultural Norms

Discussion:

Our values significantly influence the behaviors we exhibit, and the decisions we make. Values are instilled by all four components you are navigating in this guided journey. Yet, societal values reflect how we relate to our community and its standards. A person's personality is something they are born with, our patterns of thoughts, feelings and behavior that make a person unique, but many theories exist as to how personalities are further shaped—through natural, physiological and biological elements. The society in which we are nurtured can also become a significant influence on how a personality evolves.

In turn, societal values and cultural norms can influence behaviors of a generation. For example, a parent can be inspired by experts in the field on how to raise and nurture a child. If society accepts a certain parental technique during that time period, parents are heavily influenced by how that child's behavior will be reinforced.

When society introduced the concepts of participation trophies, it influenced the way some parents nurtured that virtue. In a household with several children with a wide range in age, some children were not given participation trophies, but others were. This is a prime example of how society has influenced a perspective.

This is the way that all four components are the essence of a person's personality. Society plays a meaningful part in how a person is seen and treated. Therefore, systems, policies, and theories are presented by social culture and influence people's behavior.

An individualistic society encourages individualism. This concept suggests that you are the most important thing in this world, which encourages the seeking of personal recognition and gaining your own social and financial status. While a social culture that promotes collectivism will reinforce groups as the most important thing in this world. Value is placed on the well-being of the larger group, like family, workplace, or country.

The philosophy of *individualism versus collectivism* can cause a dispute simply because of the opposing views of how person should live—individualist or collectively. A person that has the ideals of a collectivism culture may have the perspective that the individualist is "selfish." Therefore, how children are disciplined will be considerably influenced by how that society views that style of discipline.

These societal norms can have subcategories, from city to region, providences to states, and nations. All of them will be an factor in how a group functions. An example of this can be that there is the stigma or feeling that larger cities are known to be ruder, and while more rural areas are seen and felt to be more forgiving and passive (or passive-aggressive). Misinterpreting another's intentions can result from not understanding the culture in which they were raised.

For example, if a person grew up in the city and was taught that directness and clarity was a virtue of sincerity, those traits can be mistaken by someone who was not raised in that cultural norm to label the person as rude. In turn, the person from the city can become defensive of this perception because they believe they are living out an honest virtue.

Spend time to truly answer the questions in the Evaluate section of your SEED Method and then consider how you truly feel about the subject.

Activity/Assignment:

Practice the SEED Method below. If you have a current situation that you have not been willing to approach regarding this plank, practice "walking this out" here.

Things to consider:

- Do you feel that society plays a significant role in your perception?
- How has society and its standards personally impacted you in life?
- Do you believe that society has a great influence overall with people? If so, how and regarding what situations specifically?
- What cultural norms do you think have changed? What norms have not? How broad are these norms?

SEED Method	Your Perspective
STATE How is this showing up in your life? Family? Friends? Work? Marriage? Children? What is the context for you?	
EVALUATE Your opinion? Where is this coming from? Are there feelings connected? What are they? Is there more you need to learn?	
EMPATHIZE What are your similarities about this with other people? What are the differences? How can the other person feel? How is your behavior/response affecting them?	
DECIDE Do you want to modify or change? What are you willing to consider? How will you resolve any conflicts?	

PERSPECTIVE PLANK
Creativity: The Arts – Music, Dance, Artwork

Discussion:

Creativity is defined as the ability to generate ideas, alternatives, and possibilities. It is the use of imagination, new and original ideas that are typically used in the mediums of music, dance, artwork, and structural design.

Creativity opens minds and viewpoints, and can help solve problems and generate innovation. Depending on the culture, the scale of creativity can vary.

Art and Music are the representation and aspect that fully show the essence of a culture. They reflect the essence of feelings, beliefs, and values of that society. These artistic outlets help identify and preserve the rich cultural conscience that can be celebrated.

Collectively the Arts are symbols, a range of ideas that portray several meanings. Music within itself can connect and affect people like no other medium can. Music can shape a time or period; it can bring people together and make clear statements better than any other form of communication. From dance to music, from paintings to sculptures throughout history, there has been censorship and banning just because of the influence the Arts can bring. Each component can have its own distinct influence.

Activity/Assignment:

Practice the SEED Method below. If you have a current situation that you have not been willing to approach regarding this plank. practice "walking this out" here.

Things to consider:

- Is there a difference in the expression of music, dance, statues, and visuals? If so, what makes them different?

- What do you consider are expressions of the arts regarding music, dance, statues, and visuals? When is it not considered "the arts" to you?

- Have the arts impacted your life? If so, how?
- Do you believe certain arts should be more censored than others? If so, what?
- Are the arts important personally to you? What difference would it make if it never existed for you? Why?

SEED Method	Your Perspective
STATE How is this showing up in your life? Family? Friends? Work? Marriage? Children? What is the context for you?	
EVALUATE Your opinion? Where is this coming from? Are there feelings connected? What are they? Is there more you need to learn?	
EMPATHIZE What are your similarities about this with other people? What are the differences? How can the other person feel? How is your behavior/response affecting them?	
DECIDE Do you want to modify or change? What are you willing to consider? How will you resolve any conflicts?	

Naming

Discussion:

Names are a part of every culture, but the level of importance of names within cultures does vary. Names can reflect cultural values and signify a sense of pride. This topic is chosen as a plank (perspective) to be discussed because there are often extreme degrees of respect or disrespect exhibited with regard to a person's name.

A name can connect a person to their heritage, identity, and individuality. Names sometimes reflect the social aspect of a person, but it can also be a social impact ON a person. A name could affect decisions for a person, professionally, financially, and even personally.

The Inuit culture in Canada, the Northwestern region of the United States and Alaska have a powerful pride in naming. The belief is that no one really dies until someone is named after that deceased person or a living important elder. This is called *sauniq*; a word for bone-to-bone relation.

If the elder is alive when they are honored with a namesake, the two will not call each other by their biological titles, like "grandmother" and "granddaughter." They would affectionately reference each other as *sauniq*.

The importance of a granted namesake is: that it leaves the dead in peace, and prevents their spirits from being scattered all over the community. Therefore, names are not taken lightly, and giving a newborn a name is of the highest regard.

You or someone you know may be named after someone, but the reverence is not as strong. You may even know of people that are ashamed of their namesake because it can be a dated name.

There are other circumstances where there is a renaming, or the practice of having two names—one name for social acceptance, the other a nickname that gives familial affection.

The significance of surnames has bearings culturally as well. In Hispanic culture, a child will be given both their father and mother's surname. The first is the father's surname, and the second is the mother's. It is also a tradition that the woman does not change her surname when she gets married. It can be considered disrespectful if one of the surnames is dropped, as if to say one of your parent's heritage is not important.

In relatively recent western culture it has become more common for women to hyphenate their names, especially if they have established themselves professionally under their maiden name.

Understanding and emphasizing the importance of names for others can help create a sense of belonging.

Activity/Assignment:

Practice the SEED Method below. If you have a current situation that you have not been willing to approach regarding this plank, practice "walking this out" here.

Things to consider:

- How important are names to you?
- Is it important to correctly pronounce a person's name? Do you try to modify a person's name or give them an entirely different name?
- Are you okay when people call you something different than your name?
- What does your name mean to you? Do you feel there is a connection with your name? Do you feel it's a part of your identity?

SEED Method	Your Perspective
STATE How is this showing up in your life? Family? Friends? Work? Marriage? Children? What is the context for you?	
EVALUATE Your opinion? Where is this coming from? Are there feelings connected? What are they? Is there more you need to learn?	
EMPATHIZE What are your similarities about this with other people? What are the differences? How can the other person feel? How is your behavior/response affecting them?	
DECIDE Do you want to modify or change? What are you willing to consider? How will you resolve any conflicts?	

PERSPECTIVE PLANK
Transportation

Discussion:

Transportation can have an incredibly significant impact on a person's life. There are social and economic factors to transportation. The accessibility to reliable modes or means of transportation can affect a person's financial situation and impact a person's livelihood.

How people get from place to place differs by the community they grew up in—from rural, to urban, suburban or industrialized, their access to transportation affects their options and decisions.

Public transportation is less commonly used in the United States compared to other countries. Historically, public transit declined when the cost of cars dropped, and expressways linked rural areas to suburban towns and fast-growing cities. As a result, the need for public transit lessened. In other developed countries, small villages have relatively regular bus routes. In many other countries, the towns and villages were built around the transit system. Access to public transit potentially changes the economic structure for small towns.

There is reverse impact of this dilemma as well. Manufacturing plants are usually in more rural and suburban areas in the United States because of the larger footprint required. Because of the challenge of public transportation, and even some state regulations of vehicle ownership, large numbers of people may not have the means to get to work. With a concentrated population you tend to have a higher level of unemployment within larger cities, and those living in the city are less likely to own their own vehicle. Public transportation doesn't usually extend to the rural facilities for employment in those manufacturing plants. To solve this issue, some companies have created their own internal transit system to pick up people from the cities to bring them to their rural facility, but for many, getting to a job site can be a difficult hurdle.

The ownership of private vehicles mostly reflects the average citizen's income. If a person is below the average income, their ability to have reliable transportation is problematic.

Activity/Assignment:

Practice the SEED Method below. If you have a current situation that you have not been willing to approach regarding this plank, practice "walking this out" here.

Things to consider:

- Is it challenging for you to get from place to place?
- Have you ever had to be dependent on public transportation? If so, for how long? What was the circumstance? Did you have an alternative or was public transportation your only option?
- Do you know the transportation infrastructure of your city?

SEED Method	Your Perspective
STATE How is this showing up in your life? Family? Friends? Work? Marriage? Children? What is the context for you?	
EVALUATE Your opinion? Where is this coming from? Are there feelings connected? What are they? Is there more you need to learn?	
EMPATHIZE What are your similarities about this with other people? What are the differences? How can the other person feel? How is your behavior/response affecting them?	
DECIDE Do you want to modify or change? What are you willing to consider? How will you resolve any conflicts?	

PERSPECTIVE PLANK
Healthcare and Medicine

Discussion:

Culture influences the role of medicine, its perspective, and treatment. In turn, it affects decisions made regarding the usage and process. Religious groups can play the most influential role in the usage of mainstream healthcare. Medical beliefs of this level are in every country and can be traced back as early as the 1800s in England.

The approach of a medical practitioner can be different based on the belief system of that culture, and, as a result, the treatment for a patient could be significantly different. The difference is most apparent between western and non-western cultures.

Eastern cultures are more likely to include holistic treatments to heal because of the belief that all of the parts of the body are interconnected. Religious beliefs play a significant role in the level and kind of treatment a person will allow.

Activity/Assignment:

Practice the SEED Method below. If you have a current situation that you have not been willing to approach regarding this plank, practice "walking this out" here.

Things to consider:

- What medical interventions do you believe in?
- To what length will you allow medical intervention?
- Have you tried or do you believe in eastern medical practices? What about western?

SEED Method	Your Perspective
STATE How is this showing up in your life? Family? Friends? Work? Marriage? Children? What is the context for you?	
EVALUATE Your opinion? Where is this coming from? Are there feelings connected? What are they? Is there more you need to learn?	
EMPATHIZE What are your similarities about this with other people? What are the differences? How can the other person feel? How is your behavior/response affecting them?	
DECIDE Do you want to modify or change? What are you willing to consider? How will you resolve any conflicts?	

PERSPECTIVE PLANK
Political Culture – Political System – Government

Discussion:

The existence of political systems and their purpose can be vastly polarizing when it comes to people's beliefs. The opinion of how certain public processes should be managed is based on a person's set of values, feelings, and personal perspectives on political or public governance. These beliefs can lead to emotionally charged and strongly held debates. They become strongly contested because one person may feel another is denying the rights they believe they should have. And two people can have entirely different opinions about the responsibilities and powers a government should exercise.

The high probability of this plank (perspective) being the cause of strong disagreements makes it imperative to have this as a guided journal practice to process. Every person, group, class, culture, and country are affected by a society's political positions and systems.

Political systems have existed since the ancient days of Greece and Rome. Every culture has some form of government; monarchy, republic, democracy, autocracy, and egalitarian (equality) within tribal societies. Systems of government continue to evolve.

Activity/Assignment:

Practice the SEED Method below. If you have a current situation that you have not been willing to approach regarding this plank, practice "walking this out" here.

Things to consider:

- What liberties do you believe a citizen should have?
- How much should the government play a part in daily lives?
- Are there some people that should be governed and guided?
- Should the government protect, defend, and provide for its people?

SEED Method	Your Perspective
STATE How is this showing up in your life? Family? Friends? Work? Marriage? Children? What is the context for you?	
EVALUATE Your opinion? Where is this coming from? Are there feelings connected? What are they? Is there more you need to learn?	
EMPATHIZE What are your similarities about this with other people? What are the differences? How can the other person feel? How is your behavior/response affecting them?	
DECIDE Do you want to modify or change? What are you willing to consider? How will you resolve any conflicts?	

PERSPECTIVE PLANK
Laws and Enforcement

Discussion:

Laws are a system of rules created to be enforced through institutions designated to regulate behavior. The systems can vary between countries, and they can have implications for the society and individuals. In many societies, congresses, courts or magistrates make decisions about the law. In some societies, religious groups have the authority to enforce and evoke their rules of behavior on their members.

Citizens often note that the enforcement of laws is not always consistent across all members of the community. The relationship between law enforcement and all subsets of society may be quite different, causing controversy and discord. This can result in conflict because the direct experiences and associations are not the same for everyone.

Activity/Assignment:

Practice the SEED Method below. If you have a current situation that you have not been willing to approach regarding this plank, practice "walking this out" here.

Things to consider:

- Have you discussed police, law enforcement, or any civil service? If so, what are the discussions usually about?

- In your perspective, are police, law enforcement or any civil service personnel well-regarded? What are your sentiments when discussing these professions?

- Do you trust that laws are created fairly? Do you believe you can trust law enforcement?

- Why do you think laws are created? Who are they created for?

- How much merit do you place on law enforcement?

- How do you behave around law enforcement?

- When completing the "Empathize" section, try to not only empathize with a person that has different views than you, but also empathize and relate to law enforcement's viewpoint.

SEED Method	Your Perspective
STATE How is this showing up in your life? Family? Friends? Work? Marriage? Children? What is the context for you?	
EVALUATE Your opinion? Where is this coming from? Are there feelings connected? What are they? Is there more you need to learn?	
EMPATHIZE What are your similarities about this with other people? What are the differences? How can the other person feel? How is your behavior/response affecting them?	
DECIDE Do you want to modify or change? What are you willing to consider? How will you resolve any conflicts?	

PERSPECTIVE PLANK
Crime and Incarceration

Discussion:

Crime is an act that is considered socially prohibited for which the government can punish a person. Crime is essentially breaking the law—with varying level of penalties for the alleged unacceptable behavior.

Therefore, when a person has broken the law, they face a trial and, if found guilty, are rendered punishment. The trial and punishment experiences may vary by location, region, and country.

The concept of crime can be perceived differently depending on the culture in which a crime's punishment would be administered. The consequence of crime is also handled differently depending on the culture.

Prisons and incarceration are another layer added to this plank's intense viewpoint (perspective). The consequence of imprisonment can be a controversial topic, especially within the United States. The United States houses one-fifth of the world's prison population, leading to it have the highest prison population in total. Nationally, there are many factors which play a part in America's incarceration process, including socio-economic inequalities, racial identities, and marginalization of groups.

Since 2005, The Netherlands has made a steady decrease in their prisoner population, which at one point was the highest in Western Europe. They have been putting more emphasis on criminal reform, and they use electronic tagging to control criminals that have been released to rehabilitate and resume normal life. The result is a decrease in the incarceration of criminals and better rehabilitation.

Activity/Assignment:

Practice the SEED Method below. If you have a current situation that you have not been willing to approach regarding this plank, practice "walking this out" here.

Things to consider:

- Do you believe there is a common thread to what causes a person to be a criminal?

- Do you believe there are better ways than prison to reform a person in order to deter future crime?

- What are your beliefs regarding the criminal process and system? Do you believe there are universally based issues in crime?

SEED Method	Your Perspective
STATE How is this showing up in your life? Family? Friends? Work? Marriage? Children? What is the context for you?	
EVALUATE Your opinion? Where is this coming from? Are there feelings connected? What are they? Is there more you need to learn?	
EMPATHIZE What are your similarities about this with other people? What are the differences? How can the other person feel? How is your behavior/response affecting them?	
DECIDE Do you want to modify or change? What are you willing to consider? How will you resolve any conflicts?	

PERSPECTIVE PLANK
Food

Discussion:

Food can be more than nutrients provided to our bodies. Food can bring people together. If you want people to attend a meeting, have food. If you want people to complain the quickest at a conference, have bad food. Food can be a great unifier that can connect across cultures and generations.

Food can also be the gate to memories of our past. People often say that just the smell of a familiar meal can flood the memories, including where you were, who you were with, and all the details of the moment of that memory.

Traditions, customs, and etiquette reflect how sitting and gathering food can represent respect, fellowship, and honor. Food can be centered around religious events, celebrations, or commemorating and experiencing any special time in one's life.

Eating the food of your culture can also symbolize pride and the significance of your identity.

Restrictions on how food should be consumed is also heavily influenced by beliefs and cultures. Some customs believe that certain food should not be consumed. For example, Hindus consider the cow to be a sacred symbol of life and should be protected. Jewish and Muslim customs prohibit the consumption of pork. Some cultures are strictly vegetarian, and some forbid seafood. Then there are the personal convictions of vegans, vegetarians and pescatarians.

Food perceptions can also be associated with food allergens, animal welfare or environmental impact.

Activity/Assignment:

Practice the SEED Method below. If you have a current situation that you have not been willing to approach regarding this plank, practice "walking this out" here.

Things to consider:

- How do you feel about food?
- Do you feel food has the power to reflect and evoke emotion?
- Do you have regular sit-down meals with your family? How much time do you spend having meals with family, friends, and loved ones?
- Do you believe food has been mismanaged? Do you believe there is a difference with how food is viewed today versus in the past?

SEED Method	Your Perspective
STATE How is this showing up in your life? Family? Friends? Work? Marriage? Children? What is the context for you?	
EVALUATE Your opinion? Where is this coming from? Are there feelings connected? What are they? Is there more you need to learn?	
EMPATHIZE What are your similarities about this with other people? What are the differences? How can the other person feel? How is your behavior/response affecting them?	
DECIDE Do you want to modify or change? What are you willing to consider? How will you resolve any conflicts?	

Discussion:

Colors can play an important role in how we display respect and solidarity with our community. Some of the rituals can feel less consequential, such as the "rule" about not wearing white after Labor Day. Some throw "white parties" for a last gasp of wearing white before winter hits, although more recently something called "winter white" has made the former rule a bit moot.

In America, one color tradition is that wedding guests are not supposed to wear white or black to a wedding, possibly stemming from white dresses first becoming the popular color for brides when Queen Victoria wore one at her wedding in 1840. The only exception to white being limited to the bride would be flower bearers, also known as flower girls In India, the biggest color taboo is to wear red for guests at weddings. Red is reserved for the bride in that country.

Mourners and guests traditionally wear black to funerals. In most parts of the world, black is the color recognized for death and mourning, yet it is not universal. In some cultures, like Eastern Asia, Cambodia, Taiwan, or indigenous Australia, white is actually the preferred color for funerals because it signifies purity and rebirth. This tradition is also true in some African American communities.

There are also other celebrations where you are expected to wear certain colors. For example, the celebration of Easter brings the expectation of wearing bright and pastel colors. Even though Easter has a religious foundation, it has become a spring time celebration as well.

Activity/Assignment:

The choice of wearing certain colors can influence things like a job interview. That type of situation may be influenced by unspoken or unwritten rules of society, yet can have significant ramifications.

Things to consider:

- Are you self-conscious of what you wear with regard to colors for special events or occasions (i.e., interviewing, weddings, etc.)?
- Do you believe there should be a standard when it comes to attire?
- Do you believe colors can symbolize different customs? If so, what are your beliefs regarding wearing different colors?

SEED Method	Your Perspective
STATE How is this showing up in your life? Family? Friends? Work? Marriage? Children? What is the context for you?	
EVALUATE Your opinion? Where is this coming from? Are there feelings connected? What are they? Is there more you need to learn?	
EMPATHIZE What are your similarities about this with other people? What are the differences? How can the other person feel? How is your behavior/response affecting them?	
DECIDE Do you want to modify or change? What are you willing to consider? How will you resolve any conflicts?	

CONGRATULATIONS!

You have successfully completed your fifth and last badge!

*You also have completed
the entire Stage II portion of your guided journal.*

You have fully completed all five badges! This is an amazing accomplishment. What an achievement!

You have completed 38 journal entries in this section. That is a true commitment and you should be very proud of yourself because you explored and self-assessed how you behave and why. You explored how other people can see things differently from you, which is an exercise in empathy.

You did some truly remarkable work. Again, congratulations.

TIME-OUT...PAUSE

Please Pause to Complete below:

Take some time to reflect on what you have accomplished by completing the questions below:

How has each component (Traditions, Cultures, Institutions and Life Experiences) showed up in your life?

Which "perspective plank" did you resonate the most with? Why?

How can the knowledge and awareness you've gained now help you?

Stage II: Post-Assessment

"You are never too old to set another goal or to dream a new dream."
~C.S. Lewis

Looking back, you have discussed and analyzed thirty-eight perspectives that can create unintentional conflict because of the varied experiences and dimensions that can make each person unique and wonderfully different.

The purpose was to learn how your experiences and thoughts may diverge with another's point of view. To learn how to personally reflect and empathize. To create a bridge to form harmony and mutual respect by utilizing the SEED Method.

In which perspective (plank) did your level of awareness improve the most? (ex. something you were not aware of and are now)

Information about which perspective (plank) surprised you the most?

Stage III: Impact

*"Knowing others is intelligence Knowing yourself is true wisdom
Mastering others is strength Mastering yourself is true power."*
~Lao Tzu

*"We have always held the hope, the belief, the conviction that there is a better
life, a better world, beyond the horizon."*
~Franklin D. Roosevelt

The impact is the calm after the storm. It is the application of what you've learned. It is the new paradigm of showing up differently; thinking, and acting differently than you did before. This section of the book will have scenarios, activities, and challenges that invite you to think about how you will react, while encouraging you to do something different than you would have months or years ago. The goal is growth, not perfection.

The purpose of this section is for you to have better relationships, and improve communications with those you encounter. It also provides the grace to listen to others' perspectives, and engage in equal conversation so that all parties are heard.

This stage's goal is to offer an evaluation that creates new behavior. It mirrors a platinum rule path—*treating people how they want to be treated and making them feel valued.*

Conclusion

After completing this book, you will sense a transformation. Transformed by how much? That is up to you.

I guarantee how you began on day one will not be the same as when you end. There will be a journey, a transformational change.

I want you, the reader, to understand the complexity of all human beings. Your layers and levels of experience play a part in addressing issues, challenges, and how you perceive and show up in this world with others.

This book could be used over and over again, and you can have new revelations when new experiences happen in your life. None of us will ever say that we "have arrived" when it comes to empathy or humanity. There is never a final destination—just more bridges of learning to cross. Because there isn't a final destination, we are never past learning, and we are never past reproach.

Remember that just because in the past your intentions were well received, and you have the intention of being a kind person, it doesn't mean you cannot impact someone negatively by doing the same thing. A different person may interpret your actions with a different lens.

There will always be bridges to cross. Don't be afraid to advance across each time or you can become complacent. Having the courage to press on can result in a continuously positive impact on the world.

You are on the last stage! You have made it to the other side. You are not the same person that opened this book. You have persevered through some challenging questions and ideas.

This stage is designed to put what you've learned into action, and to apply the new understanding about others' differences to your encounters in the workplace and your social circles. You have learned a new technique to help your relationships flourish and to tackle conflicts courageously.

Activity/Assignment:

Before you begin this stage, pause a moment to review all you have accomplished. Write below what you are most proud of regarding navigating this guided journal.

SEED Method

"Don't judge each day by the harvest you reap, but by the seeds you plant."
~Robert Louis Stevenson

State   **Evaluate**   **Empathize**   **Decide**

STATE	State the scenario.
	Subjective Sequence of Events. (Facts)
	What is the situation?
	Set of circumstances. (Outcomes)
	How did it show up?
	What is the core context?
EVALUATE	Your opinion?
	Where is this coming from?
	Are there feelings connected? What are they?
	Is there more you need to learn?
EMPATHIZE	What are the similarities?
	What are the differences?
	How might the person think differently than you?
DECIDE	Do you want to modify or change?
	What are you willing to consider?
	How will you resolve any conflicts?

I would like to re-visit the SEED Method. I created this method to help navigate when *the crossroads of misunderstanding arise.* I realized that I could not give you, the reader, information on how to broaden your perspectives—and then not give you a tool to help navigate the process.

The SEED Method is to be used when you encounter someone having a different perspective than your own, and when a person's ideas, behaviors and beliefs are unfamiliar to you, but you wish to connect and build a better understanding of them and have them better understand you.

Now you have a "go-to" four-step process to help you. Therefore, the next time you experience someone having a different opinion regarding a topic, you can recall SEED. SEED will help you manage through your thoughts and feelings, and then also help you consider the other person's thoughts and feelings.

The goal isn't to compromise your opinion, but rather to learn about how another person's life encounters, traditions, culture, and experiences help shape their perspective—and then share yours with them. Using the SEED method will help elicit empathy, as well as enhance your communication with others.

We will deep dive a little more in how to use SEED in the next activities.

SEED Method Usage
Please Be Mindful:

When seeds are nurtured, they grow. You can't hasten a crop and cannot bypass the growth process. Therefore, understand that any effort you make in the SEED Method is towards progress. You may not see immediate growth, yet you'll be encouraged and have faith that the work is not in vain.

Component's Influence

As you journey through the activities of this next section, determine how each component could have influenced your perspective in any given situation.

Disclaimer: Remember that two people can still experience all components at the same time, situation, location, events and with the same people—but there is still the over-encompassing input of personality. No matter what, we all are uniquely designed with our own level of individuality.

PERSONALITY			
Traditions	**Institutions**	**Life Experiences**	**Cultural**
Gender	Leadership	Marriage	Societal Values – Norms
Physical/Mental Abilities	Workplace Conduct	Divorce	Creativity: The Arts
Color	Teamwork	Sickness-Illness-Disease	Naming
Hair	Personal Space	Death – Dying	Transportation
Children	Feedback – Criticism	Grief	Healthcare
Aging	Recognition	Crying	Political – Government
Religion-Spirituality	Concept of Time	Drinking – Alcohol	Law – Enforcement
Family	Education	Humor	Crime & Incarceration
Birth Order Preference		Strangers	Food
Appearance			Colors

The importance of this final stage is to practice assessing where you currently stand.

Body Odor

Scenario:

A group of students are working together on a class project. Student A perceives that classmate and team partner, Student C, has a body odor.

Student A is continually offended, and feels like Student C is "smelling." Also, Student A is questioning Student C's level of hygiene. Student A clearly believes that Student C is just "nasty."

Student A privately decides to talk to Student B regarding the concern with Student C. Student B doesn't seem to be as offended by Student C's body odor, but then goes on to say that Student E's perfume/cologne is over-bearing and gives him a headache. Student A and B are perplexed with both their dilemmas, and are not sure how to proceed with the body odor and perfume concern.

State

In your own words, subjectively and factually state the sequence of events. What are the circumstances of this situation? How did it show up or arise? Has this been going on for a while? What is the root or core context of the issue?

Evaluate

Now, how do you feel about this situation? What is your opinion? What are the initial feelings? Do you think the two students' feelings are valid? Should Student A be offended? Should Student A talk to Student C about it? Is there more that needs to be learned with Students A and C? Do you believe that Student C should have a right to express their perspective?

Empathize

How do you think each student feels? How might Student E feel about this? Do you think Student C is intentionally not practicing good hygiene, as Student A believes? Do you feel Student E believes their perfume/cologne is overbearing or offensive? Could there be things within the four components that could affect each other's perspective? For example, could there be a cultural reason to Student E's perfume and Student C's body odor?

Decide

What do you think should be done? Should they talk to the students as a group? Should they change groups? What if others are having this same issue? Should they speak with them individually? Should they just meet in an open area?

SEED Reflection

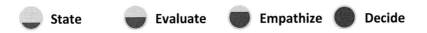

State   **Evaluate**   **Empathize**   **Decide**

This situation was a common occurrence when I was a human resources practitioner. Student A is offended by Student C's body odor and says that it is becoming unbearable to be in proximity. Student B is offended by Student E's perfume/cologne which is making them sick when they meet.

First, don't take this lightly, and second, don't jump to conclusions. These situations can be embarrassing. Also, don't downplay it, but rather address the concerns with honesty and sincerity.

There might be several reasons why there can be a disparity with what is considered "an irritating smell."

People may have body odor for various reasons, including disability. There could be a physical condition as the reason they have a presumed odor. What you find as a pleasant aroma may be completely different for someone else. There can be religious considerations, medical considerations, and cultural aspects about what is considered fragrant or odorous.

This situation can more serious and sensitive than first thought. There can be liberties regarding religion, disability, race, national origin or even gender that are protected legally.

First Step: Talk with the person to understand their perspective and situation. Don't assume they are intentionally offensive. Assume positive intentions. Generally speaking, people do not want to impact someone else negatively. Do not assume they are not following hygienic protocols or they recognize that their fragrance is unreasonable. A scent agreement could be enacted to encourage minimizing the use of scents out of respect for others. The use of scents can present a health issue for some workers or customers.

Look Me in the Eye

Scenario:

A manager and their administrative assistant have been working together for a few months now. The manager feels the team has a good relationship.

One day the administrative assistant approaches the manager and states that they feel uncomfortable when the manager speaks to them. They feel like the manager is staring at them. The manager quickly apologizes and asks when this is occurring. The administrative assistant states that it only happens with a direct conversation between the two of them. The manager asks for further clarification; the administrative assistant states that when the manager is speaking to them, the manager is looking them directly in the eye. The administrative assistant cannot determine if this happens when the administrative assistant speaks or when the manager is speaking, or both ways. The manager is perplexed because they have always been told to look someone in the eye when they are talking to them. That is a sign of respect. Now the manager is feeling very confused about the entire situation.

State

In your own words, subjectively and factually state the sequence of events. What are the circumstances of this situation? How did it show up or arise? Has this been going on for a while? What is the root or core context of the issue?

Evaluate

Now, how do you feel about this situation? What is your opinion? What are the initial feelings? Do you think the administrative assistant's feelings are valid? Is there more that needs to be learned or discussed? Are the manager's feelings valid? What is the gap? What is the bridge—the conflict that needs to be crossed?

Empathize

How do you think the administrative assistant may be feeling about this? Do you think the manager is intentionally making the administrative assistant feel uncomfortable? Do you feel the administrative assistant is too sensitive? What could cause this feeling for both?

Could there be a traditions component that is influencing each perspective? Could there be a culture component that is influencing an unconscious reaction?

Could this make a difference if the manager and employee are of the same gender? What if they are different genders? What are the positive intentions of the manager? How is the manager's behavior affecting the employee?

Decide

What do you think should be done? What modifications, changes, or considerations could be made to enable collaboration between the two people?

SEED Reflection

State　　　**Evaluate**　　**Empathize**　　**Decide**

The manager must realize that a good foundational relationship exists because the administrative assistant directly approaches the manager. Most people are conflict avoiders. The fact that it was their direct supervisor, their boss - can you imagine how this could be frightening for the administrative assistant? The manager must have established something right if the conversations occurred. It is quite easy to look at the "so-called" bad that caused a conflict. Conflicts will always arise, due to all we learned in Stage I and II. We all perceive things differently, but it doesn't mean they are right or wrong. What is healthy is to cross the bridge when it appears to yield a controlled positive impact rather than leave it uncontrolled and unmanaged.

Eye contact is an essential form of communication, however, that form of communication is interpreted differently across the world. Generally, in Western cultures, there is value placed on the ability to look someone in the eye. There can even be an unconscious level of mistrust if eye contact is avoided. In other countries, this is very disrespectful behavior. Some cultures caution to look at another's neck. Some religious groups may consider eye contact between a man and woman inappropriate, threatening, or potentially flirtatious. Yet other cultures hold that looking another person in the eye has to do with the person's status, and it all depends on the rank, seniority, or prominence of an individual. Therefore, depending on the culture, setting, and person, the message you think you are sending with the eye contact may not be received as positive. You may be wondering what you can do to make sure the person does feel comfortable.

Be aware of not fixating your eyes for long periods of time. Blink naturally, and occasionally move your eyes to another place. A smile can help—it is said to be a universal non-verbal indicator of acceptance.

Flowers to Spouses...

Scenario:

"Acme Corporation" does a wonderful job of recognizing its employees. They are known to do a great job with welcoming their new employees and especially their new leaders. Acme had a new executive leader joining the team. The long-standing protocol was to send goodie bags to children if applicable, and also a box for the executive with company logo items and apparel. A nice touch of sending a bouquet of flowers to the spouse was part of the welcome package. The same items were automatically sent to new senior executives.

For this manager, when the items arrived, the spouse received the same bouquet that was welcomed in the past by the other spouses. When the items arrived at the home, the spouse stated to the new executive, "Well honey, I guess you received two sets of gifts, and clearly I wasn't thought about and received none." The difference this time? This was the first female senior executive for the company. The new senior executive discussed this with the team and President. Some were offended that this would be a discussion. Some stated that is how it's always been done. Some were perplexed and wanted it to be discussed. A few commented that the administrative assistant should have caught the difference in the spouse's gender and made concessions.

State

In your own words, subjectively and factually state the sequence of events. What are the circumstances of this situation? How did it show up or arise? Has this been going on for a while? What is the root or core context of the issue?

Evaluate

Now, how do you feel about this situation? What is your opinion? What are the initial feelings? Do you think the new senior executive spouse's feelings are valid? Do you feel any of the senior executive team member's feelings are invalidated? Is there more that needs to be learned or discussed? What is the gap? What is the bridge, the conflict that needs to be traversed?

Empathize

How do you think the senior executive may be feeling about this? How do you think the senior executive's spouse may feel about this? Do you think the executive team and president are intentionally making the new senior executive and family feel like they don't belong? Do you feel the senior executive should have brought it up? What could cause this feeling for each party? Is there any one person responsible or to blame? Could there be something in the primary dimension that cannot be controlled or they were not consciously aware? Are there things in any of the dimensions that could be influencing the actions? What are the positive intentions? What is the impact for each?

Decide

What do you think should be done? What modifications, changes, or considerations could be made to enable collaboration between those affected? Should any new procedure be set in place?

SEED Reflection

State   Evaluate   Empathize   Decide

This is a very good example of a traditions, culture and institution component. There are many variations to this simple mistake or blind spot.

When we operate in an auto-pilot of systems, processes, and procedures, it can become very destigmatized and justified because of the repetitiveness. With the prolonged habit and behavior of doing something a certain way, it's easier to believe that doing it that way is appropriate. The comfortable repetitive behavior can create a false sense of correctness.

There is also a potential natural defense because if the sender's behavior or actions was not intentionally negative, they defend the action and avoid addressing the impact on the receiver. Having the empathy and emotional intelligence to recognize that they are not necessarily guilty, but human, is maturity. The same for the receiver's responsibility when they assume or place blame on the sender. Realizing that there was a dimension gap and a bridge to a resolution is indicative of healthy relationships and organizations. Continue improvement with behaviors, processes, and procedures by actively having conversations and utilizing the SEED Method, even in strategic planning.

I Can't Be....

Scenario:

A front-line employee has been working for the company for almost two decades. The employee is seen as a vital contributor to the success of the department and division.

The employee is a fundamental historian of understanding the company's processes and procedures.

Senior leaders have reached out to this team member for advice and guidance to help understand past issues.

Now, the employee has a new manager. Their budding relationship is challenging. The new manager feels that the employee inappropriately advises and engages with peers and leadership.

The employee feels like they are not behaving any differently than from the past. The new manager is stating that the behavior is unacceptable—and the remarks are prejudiced and derogatory in nature. For example, the former boss used to have only men take out the trash. The new manager feels all employees should rotate responsibility of taking out the trash. The tenured employee feels that only men should take out the trash—that it is clearly a "man's job."

Additionally, the employee has made comments that certain races are better employees than others and perform better. The new manager has atold the tenured employee several times that the statements are inappropriate, prejudicial and discriminatory.

The employee completely disregards the new manager and responds by saying "I can't be prejudiced because I'm a minority, and minorities cannot be prejudiced." The employee also states that because they are not in a leadership position, they can't discriminate—that only managers can do that.

Lastly, the employee feels they should not be reprimanded for speaking from their own experience. Employees are beginning to complain, especially the new ones. What should be done?

State

In your own words, subjectively and factually state the sequence of events. What are the circumstances of this situation? How did it show up or arise? Has this been going on for a while? What is the root or core context of the issue?

Evaluate

Now, how do you feel about this situation? What is your opinion? What are your initial feelings about the situation?

Do you think the employee's feelings are valid? Do you feel the manager's feelings are valid? Does any person have unjustified feelings? Is there more that needs to be learned or discussed? What is the gap? What is the bridge, the conflict that needs to be traversed?

Empathize

How do you think the employee may be feeling about this? How do you think the new manager or employees may feel about this? Do you think the employee is intentionally making the new senior executive feel like they don't belong? What could cause this feeling for each party? How could the dimensions be influencing the situation? Which dimensions and how? Are there any positive intentions? What is the impact for each person?

Decide

What do you think should be done? What modifications, changes, or considerations could be made to enable collaboration between the two groups of people? Should any new procedure be set in place?

SEED Reflection

State   Evaluate   Empathize   Decide

This is an incredibly challenging situation. The employee's behavior has been this way for almost two decades. In the past, the prior manager reinforced the employee's behavior. We all have blind spots within our experiences. Even if we have the exact same experience, it doesn't mean it will be seen the same way.

The employee is correct that the experiences they have are true to them, yet expecting it to be the truth for others is unrealistic. It is also unfair because the statements of the employee's truth can be damning and negative to others, making other employee's feel excluded and disrespected. The seasoned employee felt that they were just as offended as the employees who were offended by that senior employee.

I was hired to be the senior employee's coach. Once the employee managed through intentions (Stage I), I helped the tenured employee with the SEED Method. The final outcome: the employee finally realized they were hurting others. It honestly took a while, but the seasoned employee was able to exercise empathy.

An additional challenge with coaching the client was to process the D (decide) step in the SEED Method. The employee wanted to respond and address the situation with peers and leadership who shared their perspective, and not consider the others. The employee had to learn how to collaborate so the seasoned employee, peers and leadership felt valued.

This is a great example of being empathetic and how hard it can be if you are being hurt in the process as well. It can be challenging to determine what change in behavior you should have. All steps in the SEED Method are important to complete.

Breakroom Conversation

Scenario:

XYZ Corporation has been growing rapidly and has become a popular employer in the area. Over time the company has grown not only in size but in demographics, becoming diverse within their employee population. During break time, some employees choose to speak with each other in their first language. Other employees perceive it as rude for co-workers to speak another language, even if they are on break.

The employees that do not speak the language feel the other employees are being exclusive, and it makes them uncomfortable. The observing employees wonder if they are being talked about, laughed at, and even potentially plotted against. Those workers believe their employer should have conversations with the employees who are speaking in their native languages—and tell them to stop.

What do you think should be done? Should the workers be forced to always speak only in the dominant language of that country?

State

In your own words, subjectively and factually state the sequence of events. What are the circumstances of this situation? How did it show up or arise? Has this been going on for a while? What is the root or core context of the issue?

Evaluate

Now, how do you feel about this situation? How do you personally feel when someone speaks another language? Do your feelings change in different scenarios? Are there some languages more than others that affect you, or is it all equal when someone is speaking another language? If so, what certain ones stand out over others? Do you think all employee's feelings are valid? Does any person have unjustified feelings? Is there more that needs to be learned or discussed? What is the gap? What is the bridge, the conflict that needs to be traversed?

Empathize

How do you think the native-speaking employees may be feeling about this? Do you think the native-speaking employees are intentionally making the other employees feel like they don't belong? What could cause this feeling for each party? How could the dimensions be influencing the situation? Which dimensions—and how? Are there any positive intentions? What is the impact for each group? Does this truly impact the team or group's atmosphere? Is this always rude behavior? What would justify this being rude or unacceptable behavior? When would it cross the line? If so, what is that line? What are the factors?

Decide

What do you think should be done? What modifications, changes, or considerations could be made to enable collaboration between the two groups of people? What do you think should be done moving forward?

Should the company choose, or do you think it should be decided individually, among teams or departments?

SEED Reflection

State   Evaluate   Empathize   Decide

The most important thing is that the conversation about this should not be avoided. It would also benefit from a conversation with management. Discussions like this can be emotionally charged by both parties—so have an experienced professional who's capable of mediating the dialogue.

All steps within this scenario are important to cover and discuss fully. There should be an effective outlining of the real issues, situations, and circumstances. Being as specific as possible about the key accounts of behavior will lead to a better process of evaluating the next step. Assessing each specific situation and finding the perception and cause is imperative. When emotions are high, having evidence would be important by showing a potential video of the situation, if applicable. The goal is to help all parties be objective and see the perspective of each person.

Displaying and practicing active listening skills are certainly needed for each party in the Empathy stage. Having a moderator or facilitator to lead to the Decision is pertinent. Remember, collaboration ensures no one feels they are making concessions, but rather they feel they are being heard and valued.

Hospitality Scenario:

Scenario:

A non-profit has its team meet with an outside group to describe their organization. These meetings are typically with donors, partners, or potential clients. An employee went to the coordinator that manages food orders to discuss a private medical situation. The employee discussed they had newly diagnosed food restrictions and asked how certain concessions could be made. The coordinator responded that the food was really for the guests and not the employees. It was a hospitable gesture to be welcoming to the guests. If the employee could not eat medically restricted foods, they were to abstain, but no extra efforts will be made for them. The employee didn't feel valued, and took this matter to the next level of concern.

State

In your own words, subjectively and factually state the sequence of events. What are the circumstances of this situation? How did it show up or arise? Has this been going on for a while? What is the root or core context of the issue?

Evaluate

Now, how do you feel about this situation? What is your opinion? What are the initial feelings? Do you think the coordinator's perspective is valid? Is it all valid, or are parts of it valid? Should the employee be offended? Is there more that needs to be learned? How does this scenario make you feel overall? Could this be a common oversight or feeling?

Empathize

How do you think the employee feels? What do you think are the coordinator's feelings or rationale about the situation? Do you agree the employee should have escalated the situation? Do you feel the coordinator intentionally wants the employee to feel neglected? Could the employee have handled all this differently? What perspective components or planks are causing this disconnect between the two employees?

Decide

What do you think should be done? How should this be resolved? How should the manager handle it?

SEED Reflection

State   **Evaluate**   **Empathize**   **Decide**

It can be easy to see an offense if you are the one being offended. It can be challenging when you are functioning daily, and not noticing when you have embarked on a bridge moment. It can be extremely easy to function solely in our intentions (Stage I). Slowing down to even recognize an offense actually can be quite challenging. Remember, personalities are the overarching behavior for the four components. Some people have personalities that are very process-and-protocol driven, and less people-driven.

This may seem like a simple solution, or it may seem overplayed if you are outside looking in. The one thing to remember is: *what is common for one is not common for another.*

The Empathize step needs the most attention in utilizing the SEED Method. The key reflection and understanding are that: *when something seems very common to you, do not assume that it is very common for the other.* Responding in a defensive manner could make the matter worse than it should be. Be mindful when addressing a conflict or bridge moment, and assume the person did not intend to be offensive. Navigate under the premise that *most people* behave in a manner they believe to be respectable. Therefore, approaching in an accusatory manner won't help you connect with them. When approaching, manage your emotions, speak more slowly, and form it in a way that shows you don't assume the worst. For example, start by saying – "I am not sure you are aware that _____."

Characteristics of the Components

Activity/Assignment:

Use this. At a minimum, this activity is to help you recognize your circle. This will help you understand where your perspective may be influenced, and most of all, get to know and learn the dimensions and life of others. This is an enrichment exercise that will help you broaden your knowledge of the people around you.

Complete the matrix below, write your favorites on the list in the column titled "You. Complete the remainder of the columns by talking to one of your close or best friends, then select a person you work with, next choose someone in your neighborhood, and last, choose someone in your social group. It could be a club, religious affiliation, etc. You get to choose a favorite topic with the wildcard slot.

FAVORITES	You	Close/ Best ___	Organi- zation ___	Neigh- borhood ___	Social ___
Book/Movie					
Color					
Vacation					
Music/Song					
Sports/ Team					
Snack/Food					
Flower/Scent					
Restaurant					
Dessert					
Hobby					
Drink					
Shop/Store					
Clothing					
Animal					
Wildcard ___					

Debrief:

What are some similarities?

What are some complete differences?

What did you learn? What were some exciting reveals?

The more we get to know people, the better we can understand each other. The more insight we have, the more inclined we are to manage conflict or misunderstandings when they arise. It can help with the empathy step of the SEED Method. Challenge yourself to continue to get to know your circle of connections.

Bonus Challenge:

Now that you have some newfound knowledge of your teammate, friend, classmate, neighbor or colleague, I challenge you to surprise each of them with a gift to recognize the new thing that you have learned about them. For example— you learn that your neighbor's favorite dessert is apple pie. You decide to make them a homemade apple pie after going to the apple orchard.

Expanding Your Culture

Activity/Assignment:

Check the type of restaurants where you have eaten or food you have personally experienced from the list below. If there is food that is missing, please add it to the list.

- ☐ Afghani
- ☐ African (East)
- ☐ African (West)
- ☐ American
- ☐ Brazilian
- ☐ Cambodian
- ☐ Caribbean
- ☐ Chinese
- ☐ Colombian
- ☐ Cuban
- ☐ Ecuadorian
- ☐ Ethiopian
- ☐ Filipino
- ☐ German
- ☐ Greek

- ☐ Hmong
- ☐ Italian
- ☐ Indian
- ☐ Indian (North)
- ☐ Indian (North Eastern)
- ☐ Indian (Eastern)
- ☐ Jamaican
- ☐ Japanese
- ☐ Korean
- ☐ Lebanese
- ☐ Malaysian
- ☐ Mediterranean

- ☐ Middle Eastern
- ☐ Mexican
- ☐ Moroccan
- ☐ Nepalese
- ☐ Russian
- ☐ Salvadoran
- ☐ Thai
- ☐ Turkish
- ☐ Vietnamese
- ☐ Venezuelan
- ☐ _____
- ☐ _____
- ☐ _____
- ☐ _____

Application Activity:

Try to eat one authentic cuisine that you have never tried before.

What are some similarities? What are some differences?

What are the things that you liked? What are things that were not as favorable? Why or why not?

_____

_____

Honoring the Components of Your Life

To honor something is to have regard and treat it with admiration and respect. To do something in honor of means to pause to show recognition to the subject or person. Giving special recognition to, or living up to a commitment, is considered to give honor. How do you give honor? What is an effective way to show esteem to someone or something? When you give praise to someone, do you think of how the person wants to be honored? Do you think it matters how the person wants to be recognized— or is the fact they are being recognized enough? How to you prefer to be celebrated or recognized?

How would you define *honor*? Do you honor yourself? When? Do you think it is important to recognize others? Do you think it important to give credit to yourself?

I have asked you many questions regarding honor or respect. I have done this because a lot of times when a person or a group of people feel they have been treated unfairly, they feel it is a form of dishonor. Therefore, I wanted to closely look at what honor is before discussing dishonor.

The most common guidance about giving honor to someone is to use the Golden Rule—to treat others the way you want to be treated. If we think of the context of the four perspective components, we will realize that if we treat people the way WE wanted to be treated, they may not want to be treated that way because they are not us. Therefore, the best guidance for giving honor is using the Platinum Rule, which is treating people the way THEY want to be treated.

Is the true opposite of honor, *dishonor?* Dishonor typically means to insult. Dishonor means to disgrace or cause shame on something or someone.

Let's think about how honor can be mispresented by thinking about imitating something or someone. The old saying is that imitation is a form of flattery, but some may feel that appropriating the use of objects or elements of a culture can be dishonorable.

Using the Empathy step of SEED is best in this circumstance. Use empathy by asking someone in that culture, *"Does the use of this element or behavior bother you, or make you feel uneasy in any way?"*

Let's review a few examples.

First example; Hairstyles. If your impression that a hairstyle you see on someone is different than the culture you are familiar with, briefly complimenting the style can feel honorable; but furthering the conversation by asking deeper questions may begin to make the person feel uncomfortable and, now, dishonored. The initial compliment is honoring the cultural hairstyle, while the questioning can feel offensive and intrusive.

Let's use the Empathy step of the SEED Model. What is the purpose of further questioning? Is the questioning to enhance the compliment? Or for your curiosity? How do you think they would feel if they receive persistent questions about something that is normal to them but uncommon to you?

How to overcome this problem? First, ask for permission because that shows respect. Questioning may just over-emphasize the differences between you and the receiver of your questions, which can diminish the earlier compliment.

Next example: A person with an accent or different dialect within the same language.

The manner of calling the difference out is recognition, but may not be well-received, especially if the recognized person has been ostracized for this difference in the past. Even though it may be intended as a positive affirmation, it still may trigger a negative response in the other person.

Last example: Making note of artifacts, clothing, or certain verbal phrases that are connected to a particular culture. This can be another unintended impact, and create feelings of being dishonored. Recognize that wearing culturally recognizable clothing may not be a costume to those for whom it is a sacred homage to their ancestors. Be aware of elements of cultures that can have historical significance by researching and understanding the impact on that particular group.

Application Activity:

Assuming that someone will tell you when they feel uncomfortable is an inadequate notion. Suppose there is a behavior making someone feel unsafe, uncomfortable, or disproportionally different from others in the circle. That person will probably not call attention to the unpleasant interaction because they do not want to bring more focus on an already uneasy situation.

The activity that I want you to practice is being mindful of your actions of imitating, copying, or overly highlighting differences of others. You can do this in several ways. One, you can use the technique of assuming they were unaware of the way their comment made you feel that I offered earlier. You can also ask yourself if you are following a trend, or misappropriating a behavior or item that is historically special.

Are there negative stereotypes involved in what is being done? Are you using an item normally used as a sacred item as entertainment or fun?

Take time to learn, like in step two of the SEED Method which is: Evaluate.

Another challenge, visit venues to learn about other cultures and traditions. Attend authentic events and restaurants. Support small businesses that are managed by people who share that culture, instead of buying items mass-produced for big-box stores.

Last, talk to someone. Engage in authentic conversation. But first ask for permission to discuss things that may feel private to them. Take someone out casually and ask them if you have ever done or said something that hits on cultural issues that has made them feel uncomfortable. Explain why you are asking, so they know your intention is to gain trust, and so they can see your heart in the manner.

Discovering Others' World

The chart below has a list of behaviors. Read each behavior and determine how you would feel if that behavior was directed at you. Three relationships are listed to the right of the behaviors. Ask yourself if each person were to behave in that way, how you would feel about it?

Description:

Close Friend:
    A person that you have a close platonic relationship with, and you know about each other person's lives. They spend personal time with you, and have attended and supported you at key events in your life.

Work Friend:
    A person that you have a close relationship with during work hours. They know of personal life milestones and are social media friends. May occasionally spend lunch or a happy hour time together.

Boss:
    You have a reporting relationship with this person. Sporadically they may know of milestones or key events in your life that are mostly initiated by time-off permissions. This is the best boss you've ever had.

Place a number 1–5 in the corresponding box. Tally the score for each person.

BEHAVIOR	Close Friend	Work Friend	Boss
Tells you that they would help you with something, and at the last minute, they did not help			
Teases you about personal matters			
Tells you intimate and personal matters and ask you for advice			
Never on time to meet with you			
Gives unsolicited feedback consistently			
Consistently fidgets. Some examples are tapping their foot, cracking their knuckles, clicking their pen or popping their gum when chewing.			
Talks in close proximity to you			
GRAND TOTAL			

> **SCORE:**
> ───────────────────────────────
> One (1)
> You are not at all okay with this behavior; you are offended and feel disrespected.
>
> Two – Four (2-4)
> Use your judgment of where you are on the spectrum. Please note you can use any number between 2–4.
>
> Five (5)
> You are completely okay with the behavior and feel honored and privileged that we are conducting the behavior with you.

Debrief:

How did you feel about the exercise? Rate your feelings. One (1), meaning you extremely disliked the exercise. Ten (10), meaning this is one of the best exercises you have ever done to help identify consciousness.

What caused you to give the ranking you did for your activity experience?

Who had the highest score? What are the reasons for them receiving a higher score?

Who had the lowest score? What are the reasons for them receiving the lowest score?

Do you have differences with the three categories of Friend, Co-worker and Boss? What are the significant differences in scores? What makes these differences important to you?

What is your overall perception of the activity? Will you do something differently because of it?

How could you use the SEED method for addressing any of these behaviors?

Celebrating

Celebrating can be different than honoring. Celebrating can mean to recognize with an activity or social gathering. To celebrate can also mean to bless. The Latin root of celebrate is "to sing praises of."

Everyone has unique skills, abilities, knowledge, and experience. I like to call them superpowers. All our unique experiences make us who we are. These differences can create new ideas, as well as enhance and blend new experiences.

It is wonderful to seek to understand, celebrate, learn and recognize the unique differences of others and how it enriches a community. This is the beauty and light of how richly unique we are.

As in any light there is a shadow, meaning a darker consequence to imitating particular behaviors or customs, which can lead to unwelcomed reaction. One of the reasons celebrating differences can become taboo is when people inappropriately adopt traditions, culture, practices, customs, behaviors or attire without honoring, acknowledging or recognizing the impact of the imitation.

Start as early as childhood recognizing, accepting, and celebrating differences and, for example, celebrating the seasons. At the beginning of each season, celebrate why that season is important and different. Go to a local aquarium and/or zoo and discuss all of the differences from salt water, fresh water to the desert to rainforest, discuss all of the different types of animals and how they are important, and even learn how they can contribute to the world.

Ask the question: If these creatures didn't exist, what would happen? A great movie to reference is the movie "Bees."

Activity/Assignment:

Learn more about your own and others' superpowers. Learn about what and how your culture positively impacts the world. What would happen if that culture or tradition never existed?

Another way to celebrate is to invite families over to share celebration of their culture and tradition. Encourage and share ways they celebrate different occasions. Look at multicultural calendars or diversity calendars. Be mindful of these calendars which should include all differences: from differently-abled, age empowerment, gender influences, religions, and learning differences. Categories can also be as simple as "Left-handers Day," for example.

Being open to understanding differences does inspire the acceptance of it. It becomes a daily conversation and practice—and not an impediment to progression.

Crucial Components

One school of thought claims there are only five to six universal expressions that exist in the world. Some research claims there is only one, but on that the debate continues.

One last fun activity is to see if you can identify three common gestures and identify the meaning of the gesture that is associated with each country.

Activity/Assignment:

	Number One Things are Great Offensive	USA Germany West Africa

	Stop Insult, Rude Hi Thank you/Call Waiter	Greece, Pakistan, Nigeria Mexico, Panama USA Malaysia

	Okay Insult, Offensive Money Zero	France Japan USA Iraq, Iran

Answer Key:

Thumbs Up:
Number One – Germany
Offensive – West Africa
Things are Great – USA

Hand Circle:
Okay – USA
Insult – Middle East/Iraq, Iran
Zero – France

Open-Face Hand:
Stop – USA
Hi – Mexico, Panama
Call Waiter/Thank You – Malaysia
Insult – Greece, Pakistan, Nigeria

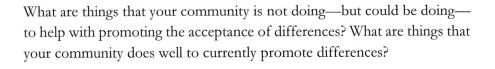

Deepening Your Components:

What are things that your community is not doing—but could be doing—to help with promoting the acceptance of differences? What are things that your community does well to currently promote differences?

In what way is your world diverse?

What are things you can personally do to promote the acceptance of differences?

Certificate of Completion

to

_____

In recognition of dedicated and continued work of strengthening relationships, within workplace, family, friends, and community by broadening their perspective and learning how to effectively communicate in a 4-step process.

Have successfully embraced the importance self-reflection, development, cultural and emotional intelligence.

Congratulations, you did it!

I truly believe in always celebrating progressions and wins. No matter how small, the recognition of growth should be acknowledged.

I say this in all sincerity, you should be proud of yourself. You made intentional efforts to lean in and learn. My hope for you is to apply this to your life, that it sparked your willingness to see others' perspectives, and for you to be courageous in speaking up to connect better with others by using the SEED Method.

I encourage you to take a picture and post your success. Please tag me when you do!

I would love to hear your story. Please reach out to Kendra Q. Dodd on LinkedIn, Facebook, Twitter and Instagram. Please tag with #Perspectives #SEEDMethod #PerspectivesJournal

Conclusion

Your Journey

"I have not the right to want to change another
if I am not open to be changed."
~Martin Buber

Thank you for deciding to take this journey. You should be extremely proud of yourself. You have done more than the average person in expanding your consciousness of learning why you may respond to certain situations in a particular way. Hopefully, you also recognized factors that can make a person think or react differently than your thoughts or reactions.

Continue to utilize the SEED Method while learning to be more present and empathetic when you encounter a challenging conversation or situation. Do not decide to take the path of good intentions. Instead, have the courage to bridge the gap and walk the SEED of collaboration and understanding plank by plank.

I have faith you will continue to be curious and courageous, and challenge yourself to learn more about yourself and others.

Please keep in touch and tell me how you are doing. You can find me on my website: www.kendraqdodd.com. You may also follow and connect with me on Facebook, Instagram, or LinkedIn at Kendra Q. Dodd.

Others' Journey

"Fight for the things that you care about, but do it in a
way that will lead others to join you."
~Ruth Bader Ginsburg

I want to discuss something especially important. The journey you experienced during this guided journal, and frankly in any part or time of your life, is yours and yours alone.

Realize the seed you are planting isn't for anyone else, this is for your development. For anyone to have the same experience you had completing this book, they must do the work just like you did. You cannot enforce learning and growth for anyone else; they must have the desire to want to discover it for themselves. The only way to really have others experience things is for them to take the journey themselves.

If you have been positively impacted by this guided journal, or any of the activities you completed, it is great that you are trying to share and influence interactions with others. You have become even more passionate about it. Remember that everyone is not at the same place as you, and may not be willing to take the same journey. Several metaphors apply, such as: "You can lead a horse to water but can't make them drink." I understand only when the reader is truly ready to be open-minded, will they be ready to learn. There is also the saying that "When the student is ready, the teacher appears."

Maybe in due time (or not), a person may embark on their own discovery journey. I am writing this because I do not want you to be discouraged—but rather to use wisdom with your patience. Don't give up on this. On the contrary, I'm advising you to be more strategic, wiser, and empathetic in action.

Final Tips and Techniques

Here are some final helpful tips I would like to leave you with:

- Always ask one more defining question or statement.

  – It is quite common to assume that agreements mean agreed similarities. For, example if a person says he dislike using a dishwasher and another agrees, it doesn't mean they agree for the same reason. One person's reason may be because of sanitary reasons, while the other person's may be environmental. Dig a little deeper to find the logic or reason for the agreement.

- Clearly define the expectation, don't use just one-word answers.

  – Don't assume that one word means the same for someone else. For example, if a team agrees on the defined behaviors that are considered respectful in a meeting, spend time to provide examples of what that is and what that looks like.

- Active Listening

  – Active listening uses all modes of communication. It recognizes verbal as well as non-verbal cues. It means not immediately reacting. It is first making sure that you pause and reflect on what has been said to you. It is listening with empathy. It is asking with open-ended questions to allow others to explain.

- You are not alone

  – Believing that you are the only person that makes mistakes and stumbles with misperceptions is not productive. Create a small network or safe village of people to discuss and communicate with.

- Remember SEED; there is always growth, but it takes time
  - Pace yourself; this is a marathon and not a sprint. Continue to move forward—the tortoise did win the race.

I welcome you now to the family, I have enjoyed my time with you. Thank you for taking this journey with me.

You can stay in touch with my website at www.fulfil2b.com to newsletters, tips and communication.

RESOURCES

Having over twenty years' experience of organizational and cultural effectiveness and norms, I had natural knowledge. To effectively author this book, I researched to verity my learnings. These are great resources and references from your journal entire perspective topics.

Beauty – Appearance

Skin Health Advanced Dermatology Center. (2021, April 1). *How Culture Influences Beauty*. Retrieved URL https://www.drsunaina.com/2021/04/01/how-culture-influences-beauty/

Givhan, Robin and Hannan Reyes Morales. (2020, January 7). *The Idea of Beauty is Always Shifting Today, It's More Inclusive Than Ever* {National Geographic]. Retrieved URL https://www.nationalgeographic.com/magazine/article/beauty-today-celebrates-all-social-media-plays-a-role-feature

Willett-Wei, Megan. (2015, August 17). *How Designers in 18 Different Countries Photoshopped this Model After Being Told to Make Her Beautiful*. Retrieved URL https://www.businessinsider.com/perceptions-of-beauty-around-the-world-2015-8

Sanders, Emma. (2018, February 4). *Different Culture's Definitions of Beauty*. *Retrieved URL* https://erietigertimes.com/1907/world/different-cultures-definitions-of-beauty/

Birth Order or Gender Preference

Vedantam, Shankar. (2017, July 4). *Research Show Birth Order Really Does Matter* [MPR News]. Retrieved URL https://www.npr.org/2017/07/04/535470953/research-shows-birth-order-really-does-matter

Guarino, Ben. (2019, March). *Birth Order May Not Shape Personality After All* [Washington Post]. Retrieved URL https://www.washingtonpost.com/science/2019/03/14/birth-order-doesnt-shape-personality-after-all/

History.com. (2019, July 22). *China Announces The End of Its Controversial One-Child Policy*. Retrieved URL https://www.history.com/this-day-in-history/china-ends-one-child-policy

Almond, D., Edlund, L., & Milligan, K. (2013). "Son Preference and the Persistence of Culture: Evidence from South and East Asian Immigrants to Canada". *Population and Development Review, 39*(1), 75–95. http://www.jstor.org/stable/41811953

Brink, Susan. (2015, August 26). *Selecting Boys Over Girls Is A Trend In More and More Countries* [MPR News]. Retrieved URL https://www.npr.org/sections/goatsand-soda/2015/08/26/434616512/selecting-boys-over-girls-is-a-trend-in-more-and-more-countries

The Advocates for Human Rights. (2019, August). *Son Preference*. Retrieved URL https://www.stopvaw.org/harmful_practices_son_preference\

Hank, Karsten and Hans-Peter Kohler. (2000). *Gender Preferences for Children in Europe: Empirical Results from 17 FFS Countries*. Retrieved URL. https://www.demographic-research.org/Volumes/Vol2/1/html/2.htm

Newport, Frank. (2018, July 5). *Slight Preference for Having Boy Children Persists in U.S.* Retrieved URL https://news.gallup.com/poll/236513/slight-preference-having-boy-children-persists.aspx

Children
Human Relations Area Files. (2015, February 12). A Cross-Cultural Perspective on Childhood. Retrieved URL https://hraf.yale.edu/a-cross-cultural-perspective-on-childhood/

Bernstein, Rebecca. (2016, July 16). *Parenting Around the World: Child-Rearing Practices in Different Cultures*. Retrieved URL https://www.tuw.edu/health/child-rearing-practices-different-cultures/

Complexion – Colorism

Flygalash. (2015, November 10). *All Around the World: Colorism in Other Cultures*. Retrieved URL https://thepowerofmelanin.word-press.com/2015/11/10/all-around-the-world-colorism-in-other-cultures/

Carson, Lindsey (Lazarte). (2019, February 2). *When People Want to Be Tan, But Not a Person of Color* [Medium.com]. Retrieved URL https://www.mendeley.com/guides/web-citation-guide

Mariam, Simra. (2017, May 17). *Daring To Be Dark: Fighting Against Colorism In South Asian Cultures* [Huffpost]. Retrieved URL https://www.huffpost.com/entry/daring-to-be-dark-fighting-against-colorism-in-south_b_58d98c5fe4b0e6062d923024

Basu, Brishti. (2020, August 18). *The People Fighting 'Light Skin' Bias* [BBC]. Retrieved URL https://www.bbc.com/future/article/20200818-colourism-in-india-the-people-fighting-light-skin-bias

National Conference for Community and Justice. (2021). *Colorism* [Online]. Available at: https://www.nccj.org/colorism-0 (Accessed: January 2021)

Concept of Time

Mastin, Luke. (2021, May). *Time in Different Cultures*. Retrieved URL http://www.exactlywhatistime.com/other-aspects-of-time/time-in-different-cultures/

Levine, Robert V. (2021). *Time and Culture*. In R. Biswas-Diener & Diener (Eds). Noba textbook series: Phycology. Champaign, IF: DEF publisher. Retrieved from http://noba.to/g6hu2axd

Pant, Bhaskar. (2016, May 23). *Different Cultures See Deadlines Differently* [Harvard Business Review]. Retrieved URL https://hbr.org/2016/05/different-cultures-see-deadlines-differently

Creativity: The Arts

Ford, Chantal. (2020, January 30). *10 Ways Music is Intrinsically Linked to Our Cultural Identity*. Retrieved URL https://www.contiki.com/six-two/10-ways-music-helps-cultural-identity/

Such, David G. (2021). *How Music and Culture Work Together*. Retrieved URL https://ccs.instructure.com/courses/1428878/pages/lecture-2-how-music-and-culture-work-together

Arts Council England. (2014 March). *The Value of Arts and Culture to People and Society, An Evidence Review*. Retrieved URL https://www.americansforthearts.org/by-program/reports-and-data/legislation-policy/naappd/the-value-of-arts-and-culture-to-people-and-society-an-evidence-review

StudyMoose. (2016). Does Art Influence Culture, or Does Culture Influence Art. [Online]. Available at: https://studymoose.com/does-art-influence-culture-or-does-culture-influence-art-essay [Accessed: 1 Nov. 2021]

Crying

Higgins, Leighanne. (2019, May 20). Japanese Hotels Launch 'Crying Rooms'. Retrieved URL https://timesofmalta.com/articles/view/japanese-hotels-launch-crying-rooms.710499

Gilchrist, Philippe. (2021, July 22). *Please Explain: Why do We Cry?*. Retrieved URL https://lighthouse.mq.edu.au/article/please-explain-july-2021/Please-explain-Why-do-we-cry

Govender, Serusha. (2021). *Is Crying Good For You?* [WebMD]. Retrieved URL https://www.webmd.com/balance/features/is-crying-good-for-you

Marcn, Adhley and Timnothy J. Legg. (2017, April 14). *9 Ways Crying May Benefit Your Health*. Retrieved URL https://www.healthline.com/health/benefits-of-crying

Sharman, L. S., Dingle, G. A., Baker, M., Fischer, A., Gračanin, A., Kardum, I., Manley, H., Manokara, K., Pattara-Angkoon, S., Vingerhoets, A., & Vanman, E. J. (2019). The Relationship of Gender

Roles and Beliefs to Crying in an International Sample. *Frontiers in psychology*, *10*, 2288. https://doi.org/10.3389/fpsyg.2019.02288

Crime and Prison

Times Travel Editor. (2019, July 21). *Shocking Reason Why Prisons are Shutting Down in the Netherlands.* Retrieved URL https://timesofindia.indiatimes.com/travel/destinations/shocking-reason-why-prisons-are-shutting-down-in-netherlands/as70317676.cms

Rigoni, Clara. (2018, July 30). Crime, Diversity, Culture, And Cultural Defense. Retrieved URL https://oxfordre.com/criminology/view/10.1093/acrefore/9780190264079.001.0001/acrefore-9780190264079-e-409

Seidler, Katie. (2011, June). *What Can Culture Add to an Understanding of Criminal Violence.* Retrieved URL https://psychology.org.au/what-can-culture-add-understanding-criminal-violence

Riep, Alexis. (2019, Fall). *The Effects of Culture and Punishment Philosophies on Recidivism: Comparing Prison Systems in the United States and Scandinavia.* Retrieved URL https://encompass.eku.edu/cgi/viewcontent.cgi?article=1680&context=honors_theses

Jacobson, Jessica, Catherine Heard and Helen Fair. (2017, March). *Prison: Evidence of its use and over-use form around the world.* Retrieved URL https://www.prisonstudies.org/sites/default/files/resources/downloads/global_imprisonment_web2c.pdf

Death and Dying

Goldade, Jenny. (2018, April 18). *How Baby Boomers and Millennials Differ in Terms of Death Taboo.* Retrieved URL https://www.frazerconsultants.com/2018/04/how-baby-boomers-and-millennials-differ-in-terms-of-death-taboo/

Cummins, Eleanor. (2020, January 22). *Why Millennials are the Death Positive" Generation.* Retrieved URL https://www.vox.com/the-highlight/2020/1/15/21059189/death-millennials-funeral-planning-cremation-green-positive

Cremation Association of North America. (2021). *Industry Statistical Information*. Retrieved URL https://www.cremationassociation.org/page/IndustryStatistics

Croteau, Jeanne. (2019, August 30). *By 2040, Nearly 80% will be cremated—Why we need to start talking about it* [Forbes]. Retrieved URL https://www.forbes.com/sites/jeannecroteau/2019/08/30/by-2040-nearly-80-will-be-cremated--why-we-need-to-start-talking-about-it/

Devlin, Thomas Moore. (2019, October 29). *Death in Translation: How Other Countries Treat Their Dead*. Retrieved URL https://www.babbel.com/en/magazine/how-other-countries-treat-their-dead

Walter T. (2012). Why different countries manage death differently: a comparative analysis of modern urban societies. *The British journal of sociology, 63*(1), 123–145. https://doi.org/10.1111/j.1468-4446.2011.01396.x

Dunn, Thom. (2017, January 11). Americans view death way differently than other cultures. This woman wants to change that. Retrieved URL https://www.upworthy.com/americans-view-death-way-differently-than-other-cultures-this-woman-wants-to-change-that

Dimensions and Components

Loden, Marilyn and Judy B. Rosener. (1991). *Workforce America! Managing Employee Diversity as a Vital Resource.* (Business One Irwin, 1991)

YMCA of the USA. (2-18, September 25). *Dimension of the Diversity Wheel*. Retrieved URL https://www.slideshare.net/ymcausa/yusa-dimensions-of-diversity-wheel

Foo, Wayne. (2016, March 16). The Challenge of Managing Diverse Teams. Retrieved URL https://culcj15020110.wordpress.com/2016/03/01/41/

Gardenswartz, Lee and Anita Rowe. (2003, April 1). *Diverse Teams as Work.* (Society for Human Resources Management).

Divorce

Steverman, Ben. (2018, September 25). *Millennials Are Causing the US Divorce Rate to Plummet*. Retrieved URL https://www.bloomberg.com/news/articles/2018-09-25/millennials-are-causing-the-u-s-divorce-rate-to-plummet

Whittemore, Jessica. (2021, October 20). *Cultural Difference in Divorce Rate and Reason*. Retrieved URL https://study.com/academy/lesson/cultural-differences-in-divorce-rate-and-reason.html

Drinking – Alcohol

Verma, Shraddha. (2021). *The legal drinking age in different countries worldwide*. Retrieved URL https://www.scoopwhoop.com/inothernews/legal-drinking-ages-in-the-world/

Social Issues Research Centre. (2020). *Social and Cultural Aspects of Drinking*. Retrieved URL http://www.sirc.org/publik/drinking3.html

Michael Savic, Robin Room, Janette Mugavin, Amy Pennay & Michael Livingston (2016) *Defining "drinking culture": A critical review of its meaning and connotation in social research on alcohol problems, Drugs: Education, Prevention and Policy,* 23:4, 270-282, DOI: 10.3109/09687637.2016.1153602

Marsh, Sarah and Eleni Stefanou. (2016, April 15). *Which Countries Have the Worst Drinking Culture?*. Retrieved URL https://www.theguardian.com/society/2016/apr/15/which-countries-worst-alcohol-binge-drinking-cultures

Novak, Jess. (2014, March 25). 10 Countries Where Alcohol Is Illegal. Retrieved URL https://www.thedailymeal.com/10-countries-where-alcohol-illegal/32514

MacLachlan, Matthew. (2016, December 8). Festive Season Warning: A Look at Alcohol Across Cultures. Retrieved URL https://www.communicaid.com/cross-cultural-training/blog/perceptions-and-attitudes-to-alcohol-across-cultures/

Education

Humanium. (2020) Situation of Children's Right to Education Worldwide. Retrieved URL https://www.humanium.org/en/right-to-education/#:~:text=Today%2C%20education%20remains%20an%20inaccessible,and%20those%20of%20their%20children.

Kahn, Suzanne. (2020, March 6). *Women With Access to Higher Education Changed America—But Now They're Bearing the Brunt of the Student Debt Crisis.* Retrieved URL. https://time.com/5797922/women-higher-education-history/#:~:text=Today%2C%20for%20myriad%20reasons%2C%20American,of%20students%20on%20college%20campuses.

The World Bank. (2019, January 22). *The Education Crisis: Being in School Is Not the Same as Learning.* Retrieved URL https://www.worldbank.org/en/news/immersive-story/2019/01/22/pass-or-fail-how-can-the-world-do-its-homework

Lumen. (2021, March). *Education Around the World.* Retrieved URL. https://courses.lumenlearning.com/wm-introductiontosociology/chapter/education-around-the-world/

Family Unit – Composition

Doka, Kenneth. (2012, February 28). *What Culture Teaches Us About Grief* [HuffPost]. Retrieved URL https://www.huffpost.com/entry/whitney-houston-death__1300060

Council on Foundations. (2021 March). *The Effects of Family Culture on Family Foundations.* Retrieved URL https://www.cof.org/content/effects-family-culture-family-foundations

Dube, Natalie. (2010). *Does Family Communication Impact Cultural Identity?.* Communication Studies Undergraduate Publications, Presentations and Projects.33. Retrieved URL https://pilotscholars.up.edu/cgi/viewcontent.cgi?article=1055&context=cst_studpubs

Food

The Well Co. (2021). *What is Food Culture and How Does It Impact Health?.* Retrieved URL https://www.thewellessentials.com/blog/what-is-food-culture-and-what-does-it-have-to-do-with-our-health

Sibal, Vatika. (2018, September). Food: Identity of Culture and Religion [ResearchGate]. Retrieved URL https://www.researchgate.net/publication/327621871_FOOD_IDENTITY_OF_CULTURE_AND_RELIGION

Le, Chau B. (2017, January 7) What Food Tells Us About Culture. Retrieved URL https://freelymagazine.com/2017/01/07/what-food-tells-us-about-culture/

Gender Roles, Categories and Orientation

Boundless. "The Cross-Cultural Perspective." *Sociology – Cochise College* Boundless, 08 Aug. 2016. Retrieved 27 Feb. 2017 from https -86/the-cross-cultural-perspective-49910465://www.boundless.com/users/493555/textbooks/sociology-cochise-college/gender-stratification-and-inequality-11/gender-and-socialization accessed January 2021

https://courses.lumenlearning.com/cochise-sociology-os/chapter/the-cross-cultural-perspective/

Ember, Carol R., Milagro Escobar, Noah Rossen, and Abbe McCarter. 2019. "Gender" in C.R. Ember, ed. Explaining Human Culture. Human Relations Area Files https://hraf.yale.edu/ehc/summaries/gender; accessed March 2021

Grief

Mayo Clinic. (2016, October 19). *What is grief?*. Retrieved URL https://www.mayoclinic.org/patient-visitor-guide/support-groups/what-is-grief

Doka, Kenneth. (2012, April 29). *What Culture Teaches Us About Grief.* Retrieved URL https://www.huffpost.com/entry/whitney-houston-death_b_1300060

American Society of Clinical Oncology. (2018, April). *Understanding Grief Within A Cultural Context.* Retrieved URL https://www.cancer.net/coping-with-cancer/managing-emotions/grief-and-loss/understanding-grief-within-cultural-context

Gross, Richard. (2018, June 6). *The Psychology of Grief: Cultural Differences in Death and Dying.* Retrieved URL https://welldoing.org/article/psychology-grief-cultural-differences-death-dying

Wojcik, Daniel and Robert Dobler. (2017, November 1). *What Ancient Cultures Teach US About Grief, Mourning and Continuity of Life*. Retrieved URL https://theconversation.com/what-ancient-cultures-teach-us-about-grief-mourning-and-continuity-of-life-86199

Hair

Stensgar, Barbie. (2019, January 4). *The Significance of Hair in Native American Culture*. Retrieve URL https://sistersky.com/blogs/sister-sky/the-significance-of-hair-in-native-american-culture

American Civil Liberties Union. (2011, March 18). *Native American Student Suspended for Refusal to Cut Hair*. Retrieve URL https://www.aclu.org/press-releases/native-american-student-suspended-refusal-cut-hair

Healthcare & Medicine

Green, Alexander. (2019, February 14). *Cultural Awareness in Healthcare: A Checklist*. Retrieved URL https://www.qualityinteractions.com/blog/cultural-awareness-in-healthcare-checklist

Koenig H. G. (2012). Religion, spirituality, and health: the research and clinical implications. *ISRN psychiatry*, *2012*, 278730. https://doi.org/10.5402/2012/278730

Guzer, Deena. (2009, February 5). *When Parents Call God Instead of the Doctor*. Retrieved URL http://content.time.com/time/nation/article/0,8599,1877352,00.html

Lupton, Deborah. (2013, January 1). *The Cultural Assumptions Behind Western Medicine*. Retrieved URL https://theconversation.com/the-cultural-assumptions-behind-western-medicine-7533

Powell, Jennifer. (2021). *Overcoming Language, Cultural Barriers in Health Care*. Retrieved ULP https://hhma.org/blog/overcoming-language-cultural-barriers-in-health-care/

Humor

Jiang, T., Li, H., & Hou, Y. (2019). Cultural Differences in Humor Perception, Usage, and Implications. *Frontiers in psychology*, *10*, 123. https://doi.org/10.3389/fpsyg.2019.00123

Leap. (2021). *Culture Shocks: Humour Across Cultures.* Retrieved URL https://leap.london/culture-shocks-humour-across-cultures/

McKeown, Gary. (2017, May 4). *Is There Such Thing as a National sense of Humor?.* Retrieved URL https://theconversation.com/is-there-such-a-thing-as-a-national-sense-of-humour-76814

Jackson, Steven B. (2012, May 18). *What's Funny?* [Psychology Today]. Retrieved URL https://www.psychologytoday.com/us/blog/culture-conscious/201205/whats-funny

Smith, Moira. (2008) *Laughter: Nature or Culture?* [International Society for Humor Research]. Retrieved URL https://scholarworks.iu.edu/dspace/bitstream/handle/2022/3162/Laughter%20nature%20culture1.pdf

Language/Education

Nations Online. (2021) *Countries and Languages. Retrieved URL* https://www.nationsonline.org/oneworld/countries_by_languages.htm

F, Tom. (2020, February 20). *10 British Dialects You Need to Know.* Retrieved URL https://www.ef.com/wwen/blog/language/british-dialects-you-need-to-know/#:~:text=In%20reality%2C%20there%20are%20almost,much%20one%20accent%20per%20county.

Khodorkovsky, Maria. (2008, November 13). *10 Spanish Dialects: How Spanish is Spoken Around the World.* Retrieved URL https://www.altalang.com/beyond-words/10-spanish-dialects-how-spanish-is-spoken-around-the-world/#:~:text=10%20Spanish%20Dialects%3A%20How%20Spanish%20is%20Spoken%20Around%20the%20World,-Posted%20on%20November

Sharkey, Sarah. (2021). *Uniquely Different: 11 Spanish Dialects Spoken Worldwide.* Retrieved URL https://www.fluentu.com/blog/spanish/spanish-dialects/

Laws and Enforcement

Cheatham, Amelia and Lindsay Maizland. (2021, April 21). *How Police Compare in Different Democracies.* Retrieved URL https://www.cfr.org/backgrounder/how-police-compare-different-democracies

Serhan, Yasmeen. (202, June 10). What the World Could Teach America About Policing. Retrieved URL https://www.theatlantic.com/international/archive/2020/06/america-police-violence-germany-georgia-britain/612820/

Lowatcharin, Grichawat. (2016, May). *Centralized and Decentralized Police Systems: A Cross-National Mixed-Methods Study of The Effects of Policing Structures with Lessons for Thailand.* Retrieved URL https://mospace.umsystem.edu/xmlui/bitstream/handle/10355/56543/research.pdf?sequence=2&isAllowed=y

Leadership

Duggan, Tara. (2021, May 18*). How Do Cultural Difference Affect Leadership Styles?* Retrieved URL https://www.bizlatinhub.com/how-do-cultural-differences-affect-leadership-styles/

Stareva, lliyana. (2018, May 29). *The 6 Different Leadership Styles Based on Culture.* Retrieved URL https://www.iliyanastareva.com/blog/the-6-different-leadership-styles-based-on-culture

Differences in Leadership Styles Across Cultures. (2016, August 4). Retrieved from https://study.com/academy/lesson/differences-in-leadership-styles-across-cultures.html.

Chamorro-Premuzic, Tomas and Michael Sanger. (2016, May 6). *What Leadership Looks Like in Different Cultures* [Harvard Business Review]. Retrieved URL https://hbr.org/2016/05/what-leadership-looks-like-in-different-cultures

Marriage

Halim, Daniel and Sergio Rivera. (2020, February 14). *Love, Marriage and Development: 4 Observations.* Retrieved URL https://blogs.worldbank.org/opendata/love-marriage-and-development-4-observations

Page, Danielle. (2017, June 30). *Why You Should Treat Marriage More Like a Business*. Retrieved URL https://www.nbcnews.com/better/pop-culture/why-you-should-treat-marriage-more-business-ncna778551

Zukerman, Arthur. (2020, May 31). *56 Marriage Statistics: 2020/2021 Global Data, Analysis & Trends*. Retrieved URL https://comparecamp.com/marriage-statistics/

Keeling, Margaret and Fred P. Piercy. (2007, October 11). *A Careful Balance: Multinational Perspectives on Culture, Gender, and Power in Marriage and Family Therapy Practice*. Retrieved URL https://doi.org/10.1111/j.1752-0606.2007.00044.x

Nationality/Citizenship

US News. (2021) *Social Purpose: Most Progressive Countries*. Retrieved URL https://www.usnews.com/news/best-countries/citizenship-rankings

Bande, Nikhil. (2017, December 26). *Citizenship – By Right or Choice*. Retrieved URL https://www.fragomen.com/insights/blog/citizenship-right-or-choice

Merriam-Webster. (2021, February). *Using 'Citizen' and 'Resident' Legally*. Retrieved URL https://www.merriam-webster.com/words-at-play/what-is-the-difference-between-a-citizen-and-a-resident

Library of Congress. (2021, March). *Fourteenth Amendment*. Retrieved URL https://www.loc.gov/law/help/citizenship/fourteenth_amendment_citizenship.php

Non-verbal – Gestures

Krys, K., -Melanie Vauclair, C., Capaldi, C. A., Lun, V. M., Bond, M. H., Domínguez-Espinosa, A., Torres, C., Lipp, O. V., Manickam, L. S., Xing, C., Antalíková, R., Pavlopoulos, V., Teyssier, J., Hur, T., Hansen, K., Szarota, P., Ahmed, R. A., Burtceva, E., Chkhaidze, A., Cenko, E., … Yu, A. A. (2016). Be Careful Where You Smile: Culture Shapes Judgments of Intelligence and Honesty of Smiling Individuals. *Journal of nonverbal behavior*, 40, 101–116. https://doi.org/10.1007/s10919-015-0226-4

Ao, Wenting. (2019, May 15). Nonverbal Communication in Different Cultures. Retrieved URL https://freelymagazine.com/2019/05/15/nonverbal-communication-in-different-cultures/

Pogosyan, Marianna. (2017, June 29). Non-Verbal Communication Across Cultures[Psychology Today]. Retrieved URL https://www.psychologytoday.com/us/blog/between-cultures/201706/non-verbal-communication-across-cultures

Bajracharya, Shradda. (2018, January 16). Non-Verbal Communication in Different Cultures [Businesstopia]. Retrieved URL https://www.businesstopia.net/communication/non-verbal-communication-different-cultures

Parenthood

Nulsen, Charise Rohm. (2021, March 29). *A Look at the Different Generations and How They Parent*. Retrieved URL https://www.familyeducation.com/family-life/a-look-at-the-different-generations-and-how-they-parent

Wheeler, Sharon. (2011, August 2). *Parenting in Relation to Children's Sports Participation: Generational Changes and Potential Implications*. Retrieved URL https://www.tandfonline.com/doi/full/10.1080/02614367.2012.707227?scroll=top&needAccess=true

Bornstein M. H. (2012). Cultural Approaches to Parenting. *Parenting, science and practice, 12*(2-3), 212–221. https://doi.org/10.1080/15295192.2012.683359

Carr, Sam. (2019, July 1). *Parenting Practices Around the World Are Diverse and Not All About Attachment*. Retrieved URL https://theconversation.com/parenting-practices-around-the-world-are-diverse-and-not-all-about-attachment-111281

Etter, Sarah. (2005, August 29). *Probing Questions: How did regional accents originate?*. Retrieved URL https://www.psu.edu/news/research/story/probing-question-how-did-regional-accents-originate/

Robinson, Jonnie. (2019, April 24). Regional Voices: An Introduction to Language Variation Across the UK. Retrieved URL https://www.bl.uk/british-accents-and-dialects/articles/regional-voices-an-introduction-to-language-variation-across-the-uk

Physical and Mental Impairments – Differently-Abled

Mental Health First Aid USA. (2019, July 1). *Four Ways Culture Impacts Mental Health*. Retrieved from URL https://www.mentalhealthfirstaid.org/2019/07/four-ways-culture-impacts-mental-health/

American Academy of Child and Adolescent Psychiatry. (2019, January. No. 118). *Diversity and Culture in Child Mental Health Care*. Retrieved from URL https://www.aacap.org/AACAP/Families_and_Youth/Facts_for_Families/FFF-Guide/Diversity_and_Culture_in_Child_Mental_Health_Care-118.aspx

The Pontifical Academy of Social Sciences. (2017, May). *The Social and Cultural Integration of Disables of People: Approach and Practices of Social Participation*. Retrieved from URL http://www.pass.va/content/scienzesociali/en/publications/acta/participatorysociety/ferrucci.html

Baxter, Cecilia and William Mahoney. (2018, March). *Developmental Disability Across Cultures*. Retrieved URL https://www.kidsnewtocanada.ca/mental-health/developmental-disability

Political Culture – Political System – Government

Winkler, Jürgen R.(2020, May 13). *Political Culture* [Britannica]. Retrieved URL https://www.britannica.com/topic/political-culture. Accessed 9 March 2021.

Moore, Angela. (2018, October 20). This Is Why Baby Boomers Are Divorcing At A Stunning Rate. Retrieved URL https://www.marketwatch.com/story/your-failing-marriage-is-about-to-make-the-retirement-crisis-worse-2017-03-13

International Encyclopedia of Social Sciences (2018, August 18). *Political Culture*. Retrieved URL https://www.encyclopedia.com/social-sciences-and-law/sociology-and-social-reform/sociology-general-terms-and-concepts/political-culture

Sparknotes. (2021). *What is Political Culture?*. Retrieved URL https://www.sparknotes.com/us-government-and-politics/political-science/political-culture-and-public-opinion/section1

Reading

Smith, Jefferson. (2015, August 18). *63% of Your Readers don't Finish Your Book*. Retrieved URL https://creativityhacker.ca/2015/08/18/63-percent-of-readers/

Gelles-Watnick and Andrew Perrin. (2021, September 21). *Who Doesn't Read Book in America?*[Pew Research Center\. Retrieved URL https://www.pewresearch.org/fact-tank/2021/09/21/who-doesnt-read-books-in-america/

Warner, John. (2016, September 28). *Yes, People Still Read. The Demise of Books Is Greatly Exaggerated* [Chicago Tribune]. Retrieved URL https://www.chicagotribune.com/entertainment/books/ct-books-1002-biblioracle-20160927-column.html

Olivares, Rodrigo. (2019, October 24). *Do People Still Read Books?*. Retrieved URL https://lifethisway.com/blog/do-people-still-read-books/

Religion – Spirituality

Pew Research Center. (2009, September 9). *Views of Religious Similarities and Differences*. Retrieved URL https://www.pewforum.org/2009/09/09/muslims-widely-seen-as-facing-discrimination3-2/

Bowling Green State University. (2021, January). *Defining Religion and Spirituality*. Retrieved from https://www.bgsu.edu/arts-and-sciences/psychology/graduate-program/clinical/the-psychology-of-spirituality-and-family/relational-spirituality/defining-religion-and-spirituality.html

Drescher, Elizabeth. (2014, October). *News Media Creation and Recreation of the Spiritual-But-Not-Religious*. Retrieved URL https://www.oxfordhandbooks.com/view/10.1093/oxfordhb/9780199935420.001.0001/oxfordhb-9780199935420-e-17?gclid=Cj0KCQiA1pyCBhCtARIsAHaY_5ehvVueuxnMmKc3GG_x1lZR1-FIzA2-SF8qpdWVp1zKKqdkYAG-0NsaArTzEALw_wcB

Self-Awareness

Eurich, Tasha. (2018, January 4). *What Self-Awareness Really Is*. Retrieved URL **https://hbr.org/2018/01/what-self-awareness-really-is-and-how-to-cultivate-it**

Menzies, Felicity. (2021). *Emotional Intelligence Doesn't Translate Across Cultures*. Retrieved URL https://culturplusconsulting.com/2015/03/25/emotional-intelligence-across-cultures/

Surana, Pratik. (2017, May3). *Is Emotional Intelligence Culture Specific?*. Retrieved URL https://www.linkedin.com/pulse/emotional-intelligence-culture-specific-dr-pratik-surana/

Gonzalez, Karin. (2020, October 4). *Cultural Empathy: Definition & Examples*. Retrieved from **https://study.com/academy/lesson/cultural-empathy-definition-examples.html.**

Senior Citizens – Aging – Retirement

Luborsky, Mark R., Ian M. Leblanc. (2003, December). *Cross-cultural perspectives on the concept of retirement: An analytic redefinition*. Retrieved URL https://www.researchgate.net/publication/8976582_Cross-Cultural_Perspectives_on_the_Concept_of_Retirement_An_Analytic_Redefinition

Lewis, Kara. (2020, August 3). *How Cultural Attitudes Toward Aging Affect Senior Care*. Retrieved URL https://www.aplaceformom.com/caregiver-resources/articles/how-different-cultures-care-for-seniors

Jacob, Liz. (2013, November 25). *What it's to grow old, in different parts of the world* [TED Blog]. Retrieved URL https://blog.ted.com/what-its-like-to-grow-old-in-different-parts-of-the-world/

Sickness – Illness – Disease

Lupton, Deborah. (2013, January 1). *The Cultural Assumptions Behind Western Medicine*. Retrieved URL https://theconversation.com/the-cultural-assumptions-behind-western-medicine-7533

Berlinger, Nancy and Annalise Berlinger. (2017, June). *Culture and Moral Distress: What's the Connection and Why Does IT Matter?*. Retrieved

URL https://journalofethics.ama-assn.org/article/culture-and-moral-distress-whats-connection-and-why-does-it-matter/2017-06

Dixon, Barbara. (2009). *Cultural Traditions and Healthcare Beliefs of Some Older Adults* [Red River College]. Retrieved URL https://www.virtualhospice.ca/Assets/cultural%20traditions%20and%20healthcare%20beliefs%20of%20older%20adults_20090429151038.pdf

Coolen, Phyllis. (2012, May 1). *Cultural Relevance in End-of-Life Care.* Retrieved URL https://ethnomed.org/resource/cultural-relevance-in-end-of-life-care/

Societal Values – Cultural Norms

Putnam, Samuel and Masha A. Gartstein. (2019, January 12). *How Different Cultures Shape Children's Personalities in Different Ways.* Retrieved URL https://www.washingtonpost.com/national/health-science/how-different-cultures-shape-childrens-personalities-in-different-ways/2019/01/11/1c059a92-f7de-11e8-8d64-4e79db33382f_story.html

Bertsch, Andy and Fillian Warner-Soderholm. (2013, September 16). *Exploring Societal Cultural Values and Human Rights and Development.* Retrieved URL https://journals.sagepub.com/doi/full/10.1177/2158244013502988

Shah, Shelly. (2021). *Values and Norms of Society: Conformity, Conflict and Deviation in Norms* [Sociology Discussion]. Retrieved URL https://www.sociologydiscussion.com/society/values-and-norms-of-society-conformity-conflict-and-deviation-in-norms/2292

Strangers – Helping Behavior

Levine, Robert, Ara Norenzayan and Karen Phibrick. (2001, September 1). Cross-Cultural Difference in Helping Strangers [Journal of Cross-Cultural Psychology]. Retrieved URL. https://journals.sagepub.com/doi/10.1177/0022022101032005002

Levine, Robert. (2003). Measuring Helping Behavior Across Cultures. *Online Reading in Psychology and Culture,* 5(3). https://doi.org/10.9707/2307-0919.1049

Taylor, Erin. (2012, September 10). *Hug, Hit or Ignore? Cultural Differences in Dealing with Strangers.* Retrieved URL https://popanth.com/article/hug-hit-or-ignore-cultural-differences-in-dealing-with-strangers

Boya, Natalie. (2013, September 17). *Prosocial Behavior: How Gender and Culture Predict Helping.* Retrieved from https://study.com/academy/lesson/prosocial-behavior-how-gender-and-culture-predict-helping.html.

Transportation

English, Jonathan. (2018, October 10). *Why Public Transportation Works Better Outside in the US.* Retrieved URL https://www.bloomberg.com/news/articles/2018-10-10/why-public-transportation-works-better-outside-the-u-s

Noussan M., Hafner M., Tagliapietra S. (2020) *The Evolution of Transport Across World Regions. In: The Future of Transport Between Digitalization and Decarbonization.* SpringerBriefs in Energy. Springer, Cham. https://doi.org/10.1007/978-3-030-37966-7_1

Voting

Interpreters and Translators. (2020, February 25). *A Brief History of Native American Languages in the US.* Retrieved URL https://blog.itittranslates.com/2020/02/25/a-brief-history-of-native-american-languages-in-the-us/

Fair Vote. (2020, October). *Electoral Systems Around the World.* Retrieved URL https://www.fairvote.org/research_electoralsystems_world

Schumacher, Shannon and Aidan Connaughton. (2020, October 30). *From Voter Registration to Mail-In Ballots, How Do Countries Around the World Run Their Elections?.* Retrieved URL https://www.pewresearch.org/fact-tank/2020/10/30/from-voter-registration-to-mail-in-ballots-how-do-countries-around-the-world-run-their-elections/